Learning Angular for .NET Developers

Developers

Build modern single-page web applications using Angular
and rock-solid web services using ASP.NET Web API

Rajesh Gunasundaram

BIRMINGHAM - MUMBAI

Learning Angular for .NET Developers

First published: June 2017

Production reference: 1280617

Published by Packt Publishing Ltd.
Livery Place
35 Livery Street
Birmingham
B3 2PB, UK.

ISBN 978-1-78588-428-3

www.packtpub.com

Credits

Author
Rajesh Gunasundaram

Reviewers
Ramchandra Vellanki
Alex Pop

Commissioning Editor
Sarah Crofton

Acquisition Editor
Larissa Pinto

Content Development Editor
Aditi Gour

Technical Editor
Ralph Rosario

Copy Editor
Shaila Kusanale

Project Coordinator
Devanshi Doshi

Proofreader
Safis Editing

Indexer
Tejal Daruwale Soni

Graphics
Jason Monteiro

Production Coordinator
Shraddha Falebhai

About the Author

Rajesh Gunasundaram is a software architect, technical writer, and blogger. He has over 15 years of experience in the IT industry, with more than 12 years of using Microsoft .NET, 2 years of using BizTalk Server, and a year of iOS application development.

Rajesh is the founder and editor of technical blogs programmerguide.net and ioscorner.com, and you can find many of his technical writings on .NET and iOS. He is also the founder and developer of a web product, VideoLens.net, a platform that analyses Facebook and YouTube videos and channels. Also, he has written two books, *ASP.NET Web API Security Essentials* and *CORS Essentials* for Packt Publishing.

Rajesh is also a YouTuber, running two channels: rajeshmgonline and ProgrammerGuide. He holds a master's degree in computer application and began his career as a software engineer in 2002. He worked on client premises located in various countries, such as UK, Belarus, and Norway. He also has experience in developing mobile applications for iPhone and iPad. His technical strengths include Azure, Xamarin, ASP.NET MVC, Web API, WCF, .NET Framework/.Net Core, C#, Objective-C, Angular, Bot Framework, BizTalk, SQL Server, REST, SOA, design patterns, and software architecture.

I would like to dedicate this book to my family and my team. I am thankful to the entire team at Packt Publishing for providing me with the opportunity to write this book. Thanks to Larissa Pinto for having confidence in me and giving me the opportunity to write this book. Thanks to Prachi Bisht, who brought me into the world of writing books. Thanks to Aditi Gour and Shali Deeraj for guiding me and helping me shape the content of the book. Thanks to Ralph Rosario for verifying the technical content and bringing it to good shape.

About the Reviewers

Alex Pop is a professional software developer with 15 years of experience in building applications for various platforms and technologies. He has worked for ISVs building enterprise resource planning applications, insurance and financial software products, a content management system, and in the higher education sector as a web application developer. He is the author of two programming books: *Learning Underscore.js* and *Learning AngularJS for .NET developers*. His developer blog at alexvpop.blogspot.com contains technical articles around .NET, JavaScript, and various software engineering topics.

I would like to thank my wife and daughter for their support and motivation.

Ramachandra Vellanki is a passionate programmer. He has 13 years of programming experience, has worked in different roles, and has experience in building and maintaining large-scale products/applications. He started his career with IBM iSeries, and then worked on C++, MFC, .NET, and JavaScript. Currently, he is working on .NET and JavaScript technologies. He enjoys exploring and learning new technologies.

I would like to thank my parents (Saroja and Ramaiah), wife (Sirisha), and kids (Abhi and Ani) for their love, understanding, and constant support. I also would like to thank all my friends and relatives for their continuous encouragement and support throughout my career and life.

www.PacktPub.com

For support files and downloads related to your book, please visit www.PacktPub.com.

Did you know that Packt offers eBook versions of every book published, with PDF and ePub files available? You can upgrade to the eBook version at www.PacktPub.comand as a print book customer, you are entitled to a discount on the eBook copy. Get in touch with us at service@packtpub.com for more details.

At www.PacktPub.com, you can also read a collection of free technical articles, sign up for a range of free newsletters and receive exclusive discounts and offers on Packt books and eBooks.

https://www.packtpub.com/mapt

Get the most in-demand software skills with Mapt. Mapt gives you full access to all Packt books and video courses, as well as industry-leading tools to help you plan your personal development and advance your career.

Why subscribe?

- Fully searchable across every book published by Packt
- Copy and paste, print, and bookmark content
- On demand and accessible via a web browser

Customer Feedback

Thanks for purchasing this Packt book. At Packt, quality is at the heart of our editorial process. To help us improve, please leave us an honest review on this book's Amazon page at https://www.amazon.com/dp/178588428X.

If you'd like to join our team of regular reviewers, you can e-mail us at customerreviews@packtpub.com. We award our regular reviewers with free eBooks and videos in exchange for their valuable feedback. Help us be relentless in improving our products!

Table of Contents

Preface

Angular is the most popular JavaScript framework. Angular was completely rewritten with the benefits of ECMAScript 6 and supports object-oriented programming, static typing, generics, and lambdas by leveraging the power of TypeScript language.

This book will help you understand the benefits of using the Angular client-side MVC framework in .NET applications. You will learn how to use Angular with current technologies, such as MVC and the Web API. The book will show you how to develop single-page applications using Angular powered by the .NET framework. It also teaches you how to organize and maintain your code and how to integrate Angular into .NET applications. By the end of the book, you will feel comfortable adding either a little or a lot of Angular to your ASP.NET projects.

What this book covers

Chapter 1, *Getting Started with Angular*, introduces Angular and provides step-by-step instructions for building a Hello World app with Angular. It also explains the architecture of Angular.

Chapter 2, *Angular Building Blocks Part 1*, gives you a detailed walkthrough of the core building blocks of the Angular architecture, such as modules, components, decorators, metadata, templates, bindings, directives, and dependency injection.

Chapter 3, *Angular Building Blocks Part 2*, explains the functionalities of the remaining building blocks of the Angular architecture, such as forms, pipes, routers, services, and observables.

Chapter 4, *Using TypeScript with Angular*, discusses the fundamentals of TypeScript and the benefits of using TypeScript to write Angular applications.

Chapter 5, *Creating an Angular Single-Page Application in Visual Studio*, guides you through the process of creating an Angular single-page application using Visual Studio and using NPM and Gulp.

Chapter 6, *Creating ASP.NET Core Web API Services for Angular*, showcases RESTful web services and the ASP.NET Web API. Also, it takes you through the process of integrating the ASP.NET Web API with an Angular application.

Chapter 7, *Creating an Application Using Angular, ASP.NET MVC, and Web API in Visual Studio,* practically explains how to use ASP.NET MVC as a backbone of Angular application and how to combine the routings of Angular, ASP.NET MVC, and Web API.

Chapter 8, *Testing Angular Applications,* dives into the process of testing Angular components and services using the Jasmine framework.

Chapter 9, *What's New in Angular and ASP.NET Core,* outlines the new features of Angular. It also introduces ASP.NET Core and discusses cross-platform development with the .NET Execution Environment.

What you need for this book

The following software is required for this book:

- Visual Studio 2017 or later
- Visual Studio Code
- Node.js 6.10.2 or later
- Angular 4.0.0 or later
- TypeScript 2.3.4 or later
- Windows 10 or later

The following hardware is required for this book:

- 1.6 GHz or faster processor
- 1 GB of RAM (1.5 GB if running on a virtual machine)
- 10 GB (NTFS) of available hard disk space
- 5,400 RPM hard drive
- DirectX 9-capable video card running at 1024 x 768 or higher display resolution

Who this book is for

This book is intended for everyone capable of developing ASP.NET Core 1.0 applications. Good working knowledge and experience of C# and the .NET framework are prerequisites for learning from this book.

Conventions

In this book, you will find a number of text styles that distinguish between different kinds of information. Here are some examples of these styles and an explanation of their meaning.

Code words in text, database table names, folder names, filenames, file extensions, pathnames, dummy URLs, user input, and Twitter handles are shown as follows: "It uses HTTP under the hood and utilizes HTTP verbs, such as GET, POST, PUT, and DELETE, to control or access the resources."

A block of code is set as follows:

```
public void ConfigureServices(IServiceCollection services)
{
    services.AddMvc();
```

Any command-line input or output is written as follows:

```
npm run build:watch
karma start karma.conf.js
```

New terms and important words are shown in bold. Words that you see on the screen, for example, in menus or dialog boxes, appear in the text like this: "In **Settings**, we can also pick which configuration we will use and which of the DNX versions to use."

Warnings or important notes appear in a box like this.

Tips and tricks appear like this.

Reader feedback

Feedback from our readers is always welcome. Let us know what you think about this book—what you liked or disliked. Reader feedback is important for us as it helps us develop titles that you will really get the most out of.

To send us general feedback, simply e-mail feedback@packtpub.com, and mention the book's title in the subject of your message.

If there is a topic that you have expertise in and you are interested in either writing or contributing to a book, see our author guide at www.packtpub.com/authors.

Customer support

Now that you are the proud owner of a Packt book, we have a number of things to help you to get the most from your purchase.

Downloading the example code

You can download the example code files for this book from your account at http://www.packtpub.com. If you purchased this book elsewhere, you can visit http://www.packtpub.com/supportand register to have the files e-mailed directly to you. You can download the code files by following these steps:

1. Log in or register to our website using your e-mail address and password.
2. Hover the mouse pointer on the **SUPPORT** tab at the top.
3. Click on **Code Downloads & Errata**.
4. Enter the name of the book in the **Search** box.
5. Select the book for which you're looking to download the code files.
6. Choose from the drop-down menu where you purchased this book from.
7. Click on **Code Download**.

Once the file is downloaded, please make sure that you unzip or extract the folder using the latest version of:

- WinRAR / 7-Zip for Windows
- Zipeg / iZip / UnRarX for Mac
- 7-Zip / PeaZip for Linux

The code bundle for the book is also hosted on GitHub at https://github.com/PacktPublishing/Learning-Angular-for-.NET-Developers. We also have other code bundles from our rich catalog of books and videos available at https://github.com/PacktPublishing/. Check them out!

Downloading the color images of this book

We also provide you with a PDF file that has color images of the screenshots/diagrams used in this book. The color images will help you better understand the changes in the output. You can download this file from `http://www.packtpub.com/sites/default/files/downloads/LearningAngularfordotNETD evelopers_ColorImages.pdf`.

Errata

Although we have taken every care to ensure the accuracy of our content, mistakes do happen. If you find a mistake in one of our books—maybe a mistake in the text or the code—we would be grateful if you could report this to us. By doing so, you can save other readers from frustration and help us improve subsequent versions of this book. If you find any errata, please report them by visiting `http://www.packtpub.com/submit-errata`, selecting your book, clicking on the Errata Submission Form link, and entering the details of your errata. Once your errata are verified, your submission will be accepted and the errata will be uploaded to our website or added to any list of existing errata under the Errata section of that title.

To view the previously submitted errata, go to `https://www.packtpub.com/books/conten t/support` and enter the name of the book in the search field. The required information will appear under the Errata section.

Piracy

Piracy of copyrighted material on the Internet is an ongoing problem across all media. At Packt, we take the protection of our copyright and licenses very seriously. If you come across any illegal copies of our works in any form on the Internet, please provide us with the location address or website name immediately so that we can pursue a remedy.

Please contact us at `copyright@packtpub.com` with a link to the suspected pirated material.

We appreciate your help in protecting our authors and our ability to bring you valuable content.

Questions

If you have a problem with any aspect of this book, you can contact us at `questions@packtpub.com`, and we will do our best to address the problem.

1
Getting Started with Angular

If you are reading this book, it is because you are a .NET developer and would like to learn how to use Angular with the .NET Framework technologies such as ASP.NET **Model View Controller (MVC)** and Web API, and legacy technologies such as web forms and web services. It enables the developer to develop richer and dynamic .NET web applications powered by Angular. Angular is an open source JavaScript framework that helps create dynamic web applications.

In this chapter, we will cover the following topics:

- Introducing Angular
- The Angular architecture
- Building a Hello World app with Angular

Introducing Angular

Let's discuss the history of AngularJS before introducing you to Angular. It all started with improving the development process of client-side web. As part of the improvement, Microsoft introduced the XML HTTP request object to retrieve data from the server. As the advanced JavaScript libraries such as jQuery and Prototype were introduced, developers started using Ajax to asynchronously request data from the server. These libraries were extensively used to manipulate the DOM and bind data to a UI in the late 90s.

Ajax is the short form of asynchronous JavaScript and XML. Ajax can enable web applications to send data to or retrieve data from a server asynchronously without interfering with the display and behavior of the page. Ajax allows web applications to change content dynamically, without reloading the full page by decoupling the data interchange layer from the presentation layer.

In late 2010, two JavaScript MVC frameworks were introduced: backbone and knockout. Backbone provided a complete Model-View-Controller experience, whereas knockout mainly focused on binding using the MVVM pattern. With the release of these frameworks, people started believing in the power of client-side MVC frameworks.

The birth of AngularJS

A developer from Google felt that there was one major part missing in the client-side MVC frameworks that existed in the market, that is, testability. He felt that there was a better way to implement client-side MVC, and this made him start his journey to build Angular.

Google supported the Angular project, seeing its potential, and made it open source for the world to use it for free. Angular created a lot of awareness among all the MVC frameworks in the market as it was backed by Google and also due to its features, such as testability and directives. Today, the Angular team has grown from a single developer to a large number of developers, and it has become the first choice to add the power of client-side MVC to small, medium, or big web applications.

Why AngularJS?

Let's discuss why to use AngularJS and what is the benefit or value addition that our application can get by using AngularJS:

- **AngularJS provides two-way binding**: Many client-side MVC frameworks provide only one-way binding. This means that other MVC frameworks will update HTML with the model from the server, and when the user changes the model on the page, the frameworks will not update the model according to the changes made. A developer has to write code to update the model according to the user action. However, AngularJS facilitates two-way binding and has made the life of developers easier by updating the model as per the user's actions on it.
- **AngularJS utilizes declarative views**: This means that the functionalities will be communicated as declarative directions in HTML to render the models and interact with the DOM to change the page state based on changes in the model. This extensively reduces the code by about 50% to 75% for this purpose and makes the life of developers easier.
- **AngularJS supports the directive concept**: This is like writing a domain-specific language for the web application. Directives will extend the functionality of HTML and render them dynamically according to the changes in the application rather than just displaying the HTML page.

- **AngularJS is highly testable**: As said earlier, one of the main mottos of the development of Angular is to introduce a testable client-side MVC framework. AngularJS is highly testable, and in fact, the Angular team has introduced two frameworks: Karma and Protractor, to write end-to-end unit testing to ensure the stability of the code and to enable the refactoring of the code confidently.

Angular 2

AngularJS is a good framework. However, it is six years old, and there are a lot of things that have changed in these six years in the web world. To accommodate all these modern happenings in AngularJS, it would have to undergo many changes in the existing implementation, and this made the Angular team write AngularJS from scratch.

At the ngEurope conference held in October 2014, Angular 2 was announced as a massive update to Angular 1 for building complex web applications. The ngCommunity was a little upset as they invested a lot of time in learning and implementing Angular 1, and now they had to redo the process of learning and implementing Angular again. However, Google invested a lot in the migration and upgrade process from Angular 1 to 2 by introducing ngUpgrade and ngForward. Once the developers started learning and building products in Angular 2, they realized the power of cleaner, faster, and easier Angular 2.

Angular 2 was rewritten from scratch. It helped us write clean and testable code that can run on any device and platform. Angular 2 eliminated many concepts from Angular 1. Angular 2 follows the standardization of ECMAScript 2015. With the recent web standardization, the shadow DOM replaced transclusion and the ECMAScript 6 modules replaced Angular modules. Angular 2 is five times faster than Angular 1.x.

The benefits of Angular 2

The following are the features and benefits of Angular 2:

- It supports cross-platform application development, such as high performing apps like web apps, native apps using Ionic Framework, NativeScript, React Native, and creating desktop-installed apps by accessing native OS APIs using Angular methods.
- Angular 2 inherits all the benefits of Angular 1. It replaced controllers and directives with components.
- Angular 2 was written in TypeScript and also, it enabled developers to write Angular 2 applications using TypeScript.

- Angular 2 is significantly faster than Angular 1. The new component router only loads code required to render a view that is requested. The template syntax enables a developer to quickly create views with the powerful template syntax.
- Angular 2 enables us to use shadow Document Object Model (DOM). Shadow DOM encapsulates CSS, template, and the component. This enables decoupling from the DOM of the main document.
- It is the simpler cognitive model. A lot of directives were removed in Angular 2 and this means that Angular 2 has fewer pieces and fewer moving parts so that it is easier to build larger applications with Angular 2 than with Angular 1.

The development process in Angular 2

Angular 2 has two development processes, namely, the following:

- With a transpiler
- Without a transpiler

What is ECMAScript 6?

ES6 is the latest version of scripting language specification. It is a JavaScript language used on the world wide web for client-side scripting. ECMAScript 6 is a great update to JavaScript language and the process of implementation of these features in JavaScript engine is in progress.

What is a transpiler?

A transpiler basically converts any specific language to JavaScript. A good example of this is the Typescript transpiler, which converts Typescript code to JavaScript.

What is TypeScript?

TypeScript is an open source programming language developed by Microsoft. It is a superset of JavaScript, and it enables programmers to write object-oriented programs in JavaScript. TypeScript is also used to develop transpiler, which converts TypeScript to JavaScript. It is designed to develop larger applications. TypeScript was developed as per the proposal of ECMAScript standard. TypeScript has features such as classes, modules, and an arrow function syntax, as proposed in ECMAScript 6 standard.

The development process in JavaScript

Before discussing the development process with a transpiler, let's look at the development process specific to JavaScript to build a web app. We will write our code in **ECMAScript 5** and **Deploy** it to the **Server**. ECMAScript 5 is the script that every browser understands today. When a **Request** comes from the **Browser**, the server will serve the script and the browser will run it in the client side. The following diagram shows the typical development process for JavaScript:

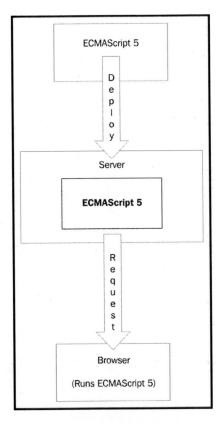

The development process in JavaScript

Development with a build-time transpiler

Instead of writing scripts in the current version of JavaScript, ECMAScript 5, we can also write scripts in **ECMAScript 6+** using Typescript and **Transpile** them into **ECMAScript 5**. Then, **Deploy** the transpiled script to the **Server**, and the **Browser Request** will be served with the Transpiled script, which is ECMAScript 5, that is to be executed on the client side.

The benefit of this is that we can use the new features of the latest version of JavaScript or ECMAScript.

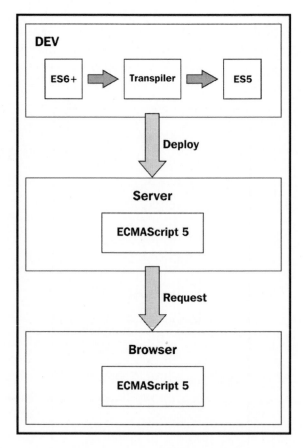

The development process with a build-time transpiler

Development with a runtime transpiler

There is another development option called runtime transpiler. In this case, we start off by writing scripts in **ECMAScript 6+** using Typescript or CoffeeScript and then **Deploy** the scripts to the **Server**. When a **Request** comes to the **Server**, it simply serves **ECMAScript 6+** code without Transpiling to the **Browser**. Then, the browser **Transpiles** the scripts to **ECMAScript 5** using a runtime transpiler to execute it in the client side. This type of option is not good for production applications as it puts extra load on the browser.

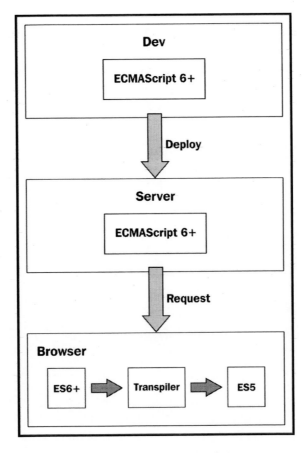

The development process with a runtime Transpiler

Transpiler options

In Angular 2, we have two options- to use a transpiler or to not use a transpiler. The following are a few types of transpilers that are available:

- **Traceur**: It is the most popular transpiler by Google, and it can be used both in build-time mode and runtime mode.
- **Babel**: This transpiler works on the most latest version of ECMAScript.
- **Typescript**: This is one of the most popular and preferred transpiler for Angular. The Angular team collaborated with the Typescript team and they have worked together to build Angular 2.

What happened to Angular 3?

After the release of Angular 2, the team decided to go with semantic versioning. Semantic versioning follows three number versioning, representing major, minor, and patch. Patch version is the last number in the version that will be incremented for every patch release, usually bug fixes. Minor version is the middle number in the version that deals with the release of new features or enhancements. Finally, the major version is the first number in the version that is incremented for the release with breaking changes.

Angular team switched to use TypeScript 2.2 from TypeScript 1.8 that is used in Angular 2. This introduces some breaking change that obviously leads to increment the major version number. Also, the current version of router module is 3.3.0, which is not in alignment with the other modules of Angular that are still in 2.3.0. So, in order to keep all the module versions in sync and follow semantic versioning, the Angular team decided to go with Angular instead of Angular 3 for their next major release.

What's new in Angular ?

The following are the new features in Angular:

- TyepScript 2.1+ is the required scripting language for Angular.
- Ahead of Time compilation mode enables Angular to compile the templates and generates JavaScript code during the build process. This helps us identify the errors in templates during the build-time rather than at runtime.
- Angular animation has its own package, and it means that you don't need to ship animation packages to the projects that don't need animation.
- Template tag is now deprecated as it leads to confusion with the template HTML tag that is used in web components. So, ng-template is introduced for templates in Angular.

Apart from these, other new features have been introduced in code level.

Why Angular for .NET developers?

The complexity of writing client-side code using JavaScript in .NET web applications kept increasing in scenarios such as data-binding, server calls, and validations. .NET developers faced difficulties in writing client-side validations using JavaScript. So, they discovered and started using jQuery plugins for validations and mostly, just to change the views according to user actions. In the later stages, .NET developers were looked after by JavaScript libraries that ensure the structure of the code and provide good features to simplify the client-side code. Then, they ended up using a few client-side MVC frameworks in the market. However, they only used the MVC frameworks to communicate with the server and to update views.

Later, a trend of **SPA (Single Page Applications)** came into picture in the web development scenario. These kinds of applications will be served with an initial page, possibly in a layout view or master view. Then, the other views will be loaded onto the master view as and when requested. This scenario will be achieved by implementing client-side routing so that the client will request a small part of the view rather than the entire view from the server. Achieving these steps created more complexities in client-side development.

AngularJS came as a life saver for .NET developers by enabling them to reduce their efforts in performing client-side development of handling applications, such as SPA. Data binding is the coolest feature of Angular that enables the developer to concentrate on other parts of the application instead of writing huge code to handle data binding, traversing, manipulating, and listening to the DOM. The templates in Angular are simple plain HTML strings that will be parsed into DOM by the browser; the Angular compiler traverses the DOM to data bind and render instructions. Angular enables us to create custom HTML tags and extend the behavior of the existing elements of DOM. With the built-in support to dependency injection, Angular resolves dependent parameters by providing their instances implicitly.

Building a Hello World app with Angular

Before we start building our first Angular application, let's set up the development environment to get started with Angular apps.

Setting up the development environment

The first thing to do before writing any code is to set up the local development environment. We need an editor to write the code, a local server to run the application, package managers to manage the external libraries, compilers to compile the code, and so on.

Installing Visual Studio Code

Visual Studio Code is one of the greatest editors used to write Angular applications. So, we start with installing Visual Studio Code. Navigate to `https://code.visualstudio.com/` and click on **Download Code for Windows**. Visual Studio Code supports platforms such as Windows, Linux, and OS X. So, you can also download it for other platforms depending on your need.

The home page of Visual Studio Code

Visual Studio Code is an open source and cross-platform editor that supports Windows, Linux, and OS X. It is one of the powerful text editors that includes features such as navigation, keyboard support with customizable bindings, syntax highlighting, bracket matching, auto indentation, and snippets, with support for many programming languages. It has built-in support to IntelliSense code completion, richer semantic code understanding and navigation, and code refactoring. It provides a streamlined, integrated debugging experience, with support for Node.js debugging. It is a lighter version of Visual Studio. It doesn't contain any built-in development server, such as IIS Express. However, it is very important to test a web application in a local web server as part of the development process. There are several ways available in the market to set up a local web server.

However, I chose lite-server as it is a lightweight, development-only node server that serves the static content, detects changes, refreshes the browser, and offers many customizations. Lite-server is available as an NPM package for Node.js. First, we will see how to install Node.js in the next section.

Installing Node.js

Node.js is used to develop server-side web applications. It is an open source and cross-platform runtime environment. The built-in libraries in Node.js allow applications to act as a standalone web server. Node.js can be used in scenarios where lightweight, real-time response is needed, such as communication apps and web-based gaming.

Node.js is available for various platforms, such as Windows, Linux, Mac OS X, Sun OS, and ARM. You can also download the source code of Node.js and customize it according to your needs.

In order to install Node.js, navigate to `https://nodejs.org/en/` and download the mature and dependable LTS (long-term support) version for Windows.

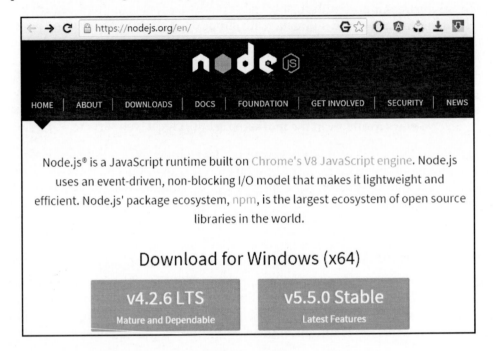

The home page of Node.js

Node.js comes with NPM, a package manager that is used to acquire and manage JavaScript libraries for your development. To verify that the installation of Node.js and NPM is successful, follow these steps:

1. Open Windows Command Prompt, type the `node -v` command, and run it. You will get the version of Node.js that we installed.
2. Now, check whether NPM is installed along with Node.js. Run the `NPM -v` command, and you will get the version number of NPM that is installed.

Command Prompt with commands verifying the Node.js and NPM installations

Now, we have all that we need to write our first Angular application. Let's get started.

Creating an Angular application

I assume that you have installed Node.js, NPM, and Visual Studio Code and are ready to use them for development. Now, let's create an Angular application by cloning the git repository with the following steps:

1. Open Node.Js Command Prompt and execute the following command:

```
git clone https://github.com/angular/quickstart my-
angular
```

This command will clone the Angular quickstart repository and create an Angular application named my-angular for you with all the boilerplate codes required.

2. Open the `my-angular` cloned application using Visual Studio Code:

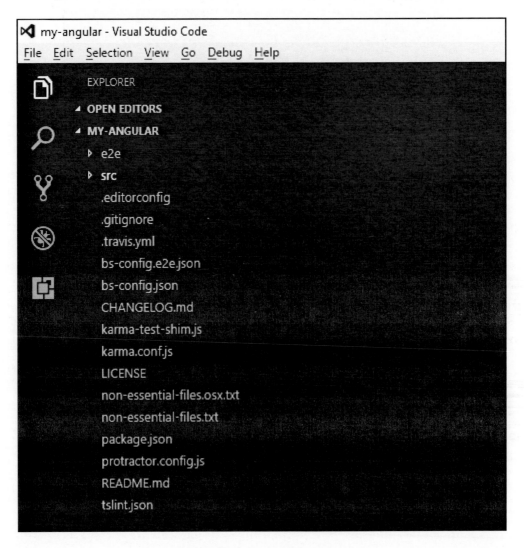

Folder structure of the my-angular application

The folder structure and the boilerplate code are organized according to the official style guide at `https://angular.io/docs/ts/latest/guide/style-guide.html`. The `src` folder has the code files related to application logic, and the `e2e` folder has the files related to end-to-end testing. Don't worry about other files in the application now. Let's only focus on `package.json` for now.

3. Click on the `package.json` file; it will have the details about the configurations of the metadata and project dependencies. The following is the content of the `package.json` file:

```
{
"name":"angular-quickstart",
"version":"1.0.0",
"description":"QuickStart package.json from the
documentation,
supplemented with testing support",
"scripts":{
"build":"tsc -p src/",
"build:watch":"tsc -p src/ -w",
"build:e2e":"tsc -p e2e/",
"serve":"lite-server -c=bs-config.json",
"serve:e2e":"lite-server -c=bs-config.e2e.json",
"prestart":"npm run build",
"start":"concurrently \"npm run build:watch\" \"npm
run serve\"",
"pree2e":"npm run build:e2e",
"e2e":"concurrently \"npm run serve:e2e\" \"npm run
protractor\"
--kill-others --success first",
"preprotractor":"webdriver-manager update",
"protractor":"protractor protractor.config.js",
"pretest":"npm run build",
"test":"concurrently \"npm run build:watch\" \"karma
start
karma.conf.js\"",
"pretest:once":"npm run build",
"test:once":"karma start karma.conf.js --single-
run",
"lint":"tslint ./src/**/*.ts -t verbose"
},
"keywords":[
],
"author":"",
"license":"MIT",
"dependencies":{
"@angular/common":"~4.0.0",
"@angular/compiler":"~4.0.0",
"@angular/core":"~4.0.0",
"@angular/forms":"~4.0.0",
"@angular/http":"~4.0.0",
"@angular/platform-browser":"~4.0.0",
"@angular/platform-browser-dynamic":"~4.0.0",
"@angular/router":"~4.0.0",
```

```
"angular-in-memory-web-api":"~0.3.0",
"systemjs":"0.19.40",
"core-js":"^2.4.1",
"rxjs":"5.0.1",
"zone.js":"^0.8.4"
},
"devDependencies":{
"concurrently":"^3.2.0",
"lite-server":"^2.2.2",
"typescript":"~2.1.0",
"canonical-path":"0.0.2",
"tslint":"^3.15.1",
"lodash":"^4.16.4",
"jasmine-core":"~2.4.1",
"karma":"^1.3.0",
"karma-chrome-launcher":"^2.0.0",
"karma-cli":"^1.0.1",
"karma-jasmine":"^1.0.2",
"karma-jasmine-html-reporter":"^0.2.2",
"protractor":"~4.0.14",
"rimraf":"^2.5.4",
"@types/node":"^6.0.46",
"@types/jasmine":"2.5.36"
},
"repository":{
}
}
```

4. Now, we need to run the NPM install command in the command window by navigating to the application folder to install the required dependencies specified in package.json:

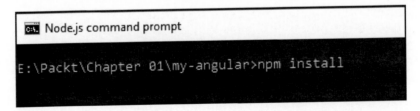

Execute the NPM command to install the dependencies specified in package.json

5. Now, you will have all the dependencies added to the project under the `node_modules` folder, as shown in this screenshot:

Dependencies under the node_modules folder

6. Now, let's run this application. To run it, execute the following command in the command window:

```
npm start
```

7. Open any browser and navigate to `http://localhost:3000/`; you will find the following page, which is rendered through our Angular application, displayed. Running this command builds the application, starts the lite-server, and hosts the application on it.

Activating the debug window in VS Code

Let's now walk through the content of `index.html`. The following is the content of `index.html`:

```html
<!DOCTYPE html>
<html>
<head>
<title>Hello Angular </title>
<base href="/">
<meta charset="UTF-8">
<meta name="viewport" content="width=device-width, initial-scale=1">
<link rel="stylesheet" href="styles.css">
<!-- Polyfill(s) for older browsers -->
<script src="node_modules/core-js/client/shim.min.js"></script>
<script src="node_modules/zone.js/dist/zone.js"></script>
```

```
<script src="node_modules/systemjs/dist/system.src.js"></script>
<script src="systemjs.config.js"></script>
<script>
System.import('main.js').catch(function(err){ console.error(err); });
</script>
</head>
<body>
<my-app>My first Angular app for Packt Publishing...</my-app>
</body>
</html>
```

So far, we have seen how to create an Angular application by cloning the official QuickStart repository from GitHub. We will cover the steps to create Angular applications in detail in the upcoming chapters. Note that the scripts are loaded using System.js. System.js is the module loader that loads the modules during runtime.

The architecture of Angular

Before we jump onto our Hello World application on Angular, let me give you a quick overview of the Angular architecture. The architecture of Angular comprises of eight core building blocks: a module, component, template, metadata, data binding, service, directive, and dependency injection.

Architecture of Angular

An Angular application normally starts with the designing of templates with Angular tags or markups. Then, we write components to handle the templates. The application-specific logic will be added to services. Finally, the starting component or root component will be passed on to the Angular bootstrapper.

When we run the application, Angular takes the responsibility of presenting the template to the browser and takes care of user interactions with the elements in the template according to the logic provided in the components and directives.

Let's see the objective of each block of Angular in the following points:

- Any Angular application will be comprised of a collection of components.
- Services will be injected into components.
- Templates are responsible for rendering the components in the form of HTML.
- Components hold an application logic that supports the views or templates.
- Angular itself is a collection of modules. In Angular 1, the main module or application module is bootstrapped using the `ng-app` directive. We can include other lists of modules that our application module or main module is dependent on; they will be defined in the empty array in `angular.module('myApp', [])`. Angular uses ES6 modules, and the functions or variables defined in modules should be exported explicitly to be consumed in other modules. The exported functions or variables are made available in other modules using the import keyword followed by the function name and then a from keyword followed by the module name. For example, `import {http} from @angular/http`.
- Each Angular library is a facade of many private modules that are logically related.
- Directives provide instructions to render the templates.

We will see each building block of the Angular architecture in detail in the subsequent chapters.

Summary

That was easy, wasn't it? We just introduced you to the Angular framework.

We started with the history of AngularJS. Then, we discussed the benefits of AngularJS and the birth of AngularJS. We discussed what's new in Angular and gave you a brief introduction to the architecture of Angular.

We also saw what is needed and how to set up a development environment in order to write an Angular application.

Finally, we did a walk-through on how to create your first Angular application using Visual Studio Code and Node.js.

We had a great start and learned a few basics in this chapter. However, this is just the beginning. In the next chapter, we will discuss some of the core building blocks of the Angular architecture, such as a module, component, template, and directive. Let's get the ball rolling!

2

Angular Building Blocks - Part 1

This chapter gives you a detailed walk through the core building blocks of the Angular architecture.

In this chapter, we will cover the following topics:

- Modules
- Components
- Decorators and metadata
- Templates
- Bindings
- Directives
- Dependency injection

Modules (NgModules)

A module is a single unit of implementation of distinct functionalities. Collections of such modules will be used to implement complex applications. Implementing module patterns helps you avoid global collisions of variables and methods. JavaScript encapsulates both private and public methods under a single object by implementing a modular pattern. The modular pattern achieves encapsulation using closure in JavaScript. JavaScript doesn't support access modifiers; however, the same effect can be achieved using function scopes. All Angular applications are modular in nature. We develop Angular applications by creating many modules. We develop modules to encapsulate functionalities that are independent and have one responsibility. A module exports the classes available in that module. Angular modules are called as `NgModules`. At least one Angular module will be present in any Angular application: a root module, which will represented as `AppModule`. `AppModule` is a class decorated with `@NgModule`.

The following code snippet shows an `AppModule` class:

```
import { NgModule }        from '@angular/core';
import { BrowserModule } from '@angular/platform-browser';
@NgModule({
    imports:        [ BrowserModule ],
    providers:      [ Logger ],
    declarations: [ AppComponent ],
    exports:        [ AppComponent ],
    bootstrap:      [ AppComponent ]
})
export class AppModule { }
```

In the preceding code, an `NgModule` imported from `@angular/core` is decorated to the `AppModule` class. Note that `NgModule` has some important properties, such as imports, exports, providers, declarations, and bootstrap.

The metadata declarations should be assigned with view classes such as components, directives, and pipes that belong to this module. The metadata exports will be assigned with the components, directives, or pipes that are usable in the component templates. The metadata imports should be assigned with the exported classes that are used by component templates. The metadata providers will be assigned with the services that are used or accessed in the entire application. It creates the instance of services assigned and adds to the global collection of services so that the services will be ready to be consumed across the Angular application. The metadata bootstrap is assigned with the root component that is responsible to render the main view of the application.

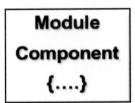

The Angular module

A sample `AppComponent` class is shown as follows. The export statement exposes the component, and the `AppComponent` class is accessible to other modules in the application:

```
export class AppComponent { }
```

A class is a template that contains definitions of methods and variables of an object. An object is an instance of the class, so it can hold the real value of the variables, and the methods can perform actions against the actual values. Note that the current version of JavaScript doesn't support classes. It's a class-free language. In JavaScript, everything is an object, and functions are used to mimic classes. ECMAScript 6 introduces syntactic sugar over JavaScript prototype-based inheritance by introducing classes to JavaScript.

Here, we leverage the power of TypeScript as a superset of JavaScript. The export keyword in the statement says that we are exporting or exposing an `AppComponent` class to other modules of the application.

Let's consider that we have saved this component in a file named `app.component.ts`. In order to access or reference the `AppComponent` class that is exposed, we need to import it in the file we will access. The following statement does this:

```
import {AppComponent} from './app.component';
```

Here, the import keyword in the statement means that we are importing a class that is exposed: `AppComponent`. The `from` keyword represents or refers to the file or module where the importing component exists. For example, it is `app.component.ts` in our case. A module name is the filename of the component without the extension; so, here the module name is `app.component`. We start the module's filename with the relative file path (`./`), and it represents the same folder.

Modules can also have a collection of other modules and such modules are known as library modules. Angular itself has many library modules. Some library modules are core, common, router, and so on. We import `Component` from the `@angular/core` library module, which is the primary module that we use for most things:

```
import {Component} from '@angular/core';
```

All Angular library modules will be mentioned without any relative file path in the from clause.

Components

AngularJS has controllers, scopes, and directives to deal with views, bind data, and respond to events by updating changes to data. In Angular, Components replaced controllers, scopes, and directives from AngularJS.

Angular, introduced components that support the object-oriented component model to write cleaner code. A component is a simple class that holds the logic of managing the associated template or view. A simple component class is given as follows:

```
Class FirstComponent {
}
```

In a component class, we will expose properties and methods to a template or view. Component properties can provide data for a template or view and allow the user to modify property values. Component methods can be called according to user actions over the view.

```
export class FirstComponent {
    name: string;
  constructor() {
    this.name = 'Rajesh Gunasundaram'
  }
  getGreetingPhrase () {
    return 'Hello Author,';
  }
}
```

The Angular component FirstComponent

As you can see, the preceding code creates a simple JavaScript class named **FirstComponent**. You may be wondering how a JavaScript plain class can be treated as a component and how a template can be wired up to this class. In order to achieve this, Angular leverages the syntax of TypeScript to annotate the **FirstComponent** class as per ES6 specification 2015. The following code shows the component class with an annotation that declares the class as a component and wires up the template with the markup identifier in the selector:

```
import { Component } from '@angular/core';
@Component({
  selector: 'first-component',
  template: `<h1>{{getGreetingPhrase()}} {{name}}</h1>`,
})
export class FirstComponent {
  name: string;
  constructor() {
  this.name = 'Rajesh Gunasundaram';
}
getGreetingPhrase() {
  return 'Hello Author,';
}
}
```

There is also another metadata named template that defines the inline template that has the HTML snippet for the view or template. The inline markup will access the properties and methods defined in the component. So here, the inline view will access the `getGreetingPhrase()` function to fetch and display the phrase to greet, and it will also access the name property to display the name. The `@Component()` preceding the `FirstComponent` class is the annotation that denotes this class is a Component, and the markup identifier first component for this component is assigned to the metadata of `@Component` named selector.

You might be surprised to see that we have not used `$scope` to expose the property and method of `FirstComponent`. Here, our component gets instantiated and is available in the template or view. So, we can access any property of that instance; also, we can call methods in the instance according to user actions or input in the view or template. The component instance provides the encapsulated data pertaining to that instance that is similar to the isolated scope in AngularJS.

Inheritance of components can happen in Angular when the template of the root component has the special tags of another component's selector, and this also enables the child component to access its parents and siblings.

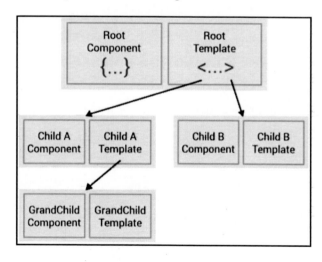

The application's component hierarchy

The life cycle of a component

Angular manages the life cycle of a component. Angular takes care of creating and rendering the components and their children and destroying them before removing them from the DOM. Angular keeps track of the value of the component property value. The following are the life cycle events of an Angular component given in calling order:

- **OnChanges**: This event is fired when a binding values changes. This method will have access to both the old value and the new value.
- **OnInit**: This event is fired after the execution of the `OnChanges` event due to binding value changes.
- **DoCheck**: This event is fired for every change detected, and developers can write custom logic to check for the property changed.
- **AfterContentInit**: This event will be fired when the directive's content has been completely initialized.
- **AfterContentChecked**: This event will be fired after a directive's content has been checked.
- **AfterViewInit**: This event will be fired when the component's template has been completely initialized.
- **AfterViewChecked**: This event will be fired after the component's template has been checked.
- **OnDestroy**: This event will be fired before destroying the directive or component.

You can either implement all of these events or only the specific events that are required for your component.

Decorators and metadata

As you saw in the last section, we define JavaScript plain classes for a component, and we annotate it with some information to inform the Angular framework that this class is a component.

We leverage the Typescript syntax and attach the classes with metadata using the decorator feature. To make a class as a component, we add the `@Component` decorator, as shown in the following code:

```
@Component({...})
export class FirstComponent {...}
```

As you can see, the code snippet shows that the `FirstComponent` class has been decorated as a component.

Now, let's attach metadata to the `FirstComponent` class using the decorator syntax:

```
@Component({
    selector: 'first-component',
    templateUrl: 'app/first.component.html'
})
export class FirstComponent {...}
```

Here, we have added metadata, such as a selector and `templateUrl`. The selector metadata configured in the component tells Angular to create the instance of a component when it encounters the `<first-controller>` markup:

```
<first-controller></first-controller>
```

The `templateUrl` provides a URL of the template file for the component to render. When you run the application, the `<first-controller>` tag will be replaced by the content of the template that is referred to in `templateUrl`. This metadata is actually a parameter to the `@Component` decorator, and the decorator is a function.

By adding metadata via decorators, we are actually telling Angular what to do with the defined class. The component, template, and metadata together constitute a view.

Templates

You will have noted that we have added inline markups for a view or template when annotating the component. We can also add a template URL isolating the view, or template markups in a separate HTML file, instead of having it as an inline view or template.

A template comprises HTML tags that provide information to Angular on rendering the components. A simple template content is given in the following lines of code. It renders the name of the book and publisher:

```
<div>
    The Name of the book is {{bookName}} and is published by {{pubName}}.
</div>
```

Inline templates

An inline template is used when there is a need to render very simple content, such as a one-liner, for example. In such cases, inline views or templates will be defined directly in the annotation:

```
@Component({
  selector: 'first-component',
  template: "<div>{{getGreetingPhrase()}} {{name}}</div>"
})
```

Isolated templates

Isolated templates are used mostly when the template contains more contents. In such cases, rather than assigning the larger content as an inline view, the content will be moved to a separate file and the HTML file URL will be assigned to `templateUrl`, as follows:

```
@Component({
  selector: 'first-component',
  templateUrl: FirstPage.html'
})
```

The local template variable

Angular permits creating template-scoped variables to move data across the elements in a template:

```
<div *ngFor="let todo of todos">
  <todo-item [todo]="todo"></todo-item>
</div>
```

In the preceding template markup, we have declared a local variable, todo, using the let keyword. Then, we iterate through the collection variable todos; each todo item gets assigned to todo and is available for use in `<todo-item>`.

A local template variable can also be used to hold the DOM element. The following code shows that the author will hold the input element itself, and the value of the element can be accessed using author.value:

```
<!-- author refers to input element and passes its `value`to the event
handler -->
<input #author placeholder="Author Name">
<button (click)="updateAuthor(author.value)">Update</button>
```

Binding

The binding technique will enable you to bind data to a template and will allow users to interact with the bound data. The Angular binding framework takes care of rendering the data to a view and updating it as per user actions over the view.

The following screenshot gives you a quick glimpse of the various binding techniques in Angular. We will go through each binding technique in detail:

```
index.html  dist
        <!-- Interpolation -->
        <div>Hello, {{authorName}}!</div>

        <!-- Property Binding -->
        <div [hidden]="hidePubName">Packt Publishing</div>

        <!-- Event Binding -->
        <button (click)="submitChapter()">submit Chapter</button>

        <!-- Bubbling Event Binding -->
        <div (^click)="reviewChapter()">
          <span>Click here to review Chapter</span> <!-- parent div handles the click -->
        </div>

        <!-- Local Variable -->
        <input type="text" #authorName />
        <span>{{authorName.value}}</span>

        <!-- Template Binding (ng-for, ng-if, etc...) -->
        <ul>
            <li *ng-for="#book of books">{{book.title}}</li>
```

Various binding syntaxes

One-way binding

Binding types such as `Interpolation`, `Property`, `Attribute`, `Class`, and `Style` support one-way data flow from the data source (exposed from the component) to a view or template. Template markups that let the data flow from a component property or method to a template are given in the following table (one-way binding):

Template code	Description
`{{expression}}`	This displays the expression built from the data source
`[target] = "expression"`	This assigns the expression of a data source to the target property
`bind-target = "expression"`	This assigns the expression of a data source to the bind-target attribute

Template markups that let data flow from a template to a component property or method are given in the following table (one-way binding):

Template code	Description
`(target) = "statement"`	This assigns the expression of a data source to a target property
`on-target = "statement"`	This assigns the expression of a data source to a bind-target attribute

Interpolation binding

Interpolation is one of the main features of Angular. You can interpolate any property value or expression to the content of any HTML element, such as `div` and `li`. You can achieve this with the help of double-curly braces, `{{and}}`, as shown in the following line of code:

```
<div>Hello, {{authorName}}!</div>
```

Here, we interpolate `authorName` to the content of the `div` tag. This is a one-way binding where the data flows from the component property or method to the template.

Property binding

Property binding is used to bind a component property to an HTML element property:

```
<div [hidden]="hidePubName>Packt Publishing</div>
```

The preceding code snippet binds the `hidePubName` component property to the `div` property hidden. This is also a one-way binding where the data flows from a component property to a template.

Event binding

HTML elements have various DOM events that will be fired when an event is triggered. For example, a button will fire a click event when it is clicked on. We hook an event listener to get notified whenever an event is fired:

```
<button (click)="doSomething()">Do Something</button>
```

The preceding Angular code snippet that wraps the event name in brackets needs to hook the event listener so that it gets called when a click event is fired.

Two-way binding

Angular has removed a core feature from its framework, which was one main reason for the birth of AngularJS, that is, two-way binding. So, two way binding is not available by default. Now, let's see how to implement a two-way binding in Angular.

Angular combined property and event binding for us to implement two-way binding, as shown in the following line of code:

```
<input [(ngModel)]="authorName">
```

The code snippet shows that `ngModel` is wrapped with parentheses and then with square brackets. The parentheses indicate that the component property is tied up with the ngChange event, and the square brackets indicate that the component property is assigned to a value property of the input element. So, when the value of the input element changes, it fires up the change event that eventually updates `authorName` with the new value from the event object. `ngModel` in the markup is the built-in directive in Angular that unifies property and event binding.

Template markup that helps data flow in both ways, from a template to a component and from a component to a template, is given in the following table (two-way binding):

Template code	Description
`[(target)]="expression"`	This assigns the expression of a data source to a target property
`bindon-target = "expression"`	This assigns the expression of a data source to a bind-target attribute

Directives

We walked through the Angular component and the way it is decorated. The `@Component` itself is a directive with a template configured in the metadata. So, a directive is a component without a template, and `@directive` is used in Typescript to attach metadata to it.

Structural directives

Structural directives deal with modifying elements in the DOM by adding new elements, removing existing elements, and replacing existing elements with new elements. The following markup shows two structural directives: `*ngFor` and `*ngIf`:

```
<div *ngFor="#todo of todos"></div>
<todo-item *ngIf="selectedTodo"></todo-item>
```

`*ngFor` iterates through each item in the todos collection and adds a `div` tag for each item. And `*ngIf` renders `<todo-item>` only if selectedTodo is available.

Attribute directives

An attribute directive will be added like an attribute to existing HTML elements, and this can alter or extend the behavior of HTML elements. For example, an ngModel directive, if added to an input element, will extend it by updating its value property and also by responding to change events:

```
<input [(ngModel)]="author.name">
```

We can also write our own directives apart from using existing ones, such as `ngSwitch`, `ngStyles`, and `ngClass`.

Dependency injection

Dependency injection is a design pattern that handles dependencies and resolves them. An instance of the dependencies will be passed to the dependent in order to use it. If a client module or class is dependent on a service, it needs to create an instance of the service before using it. We can inject or pass the instance of the service to the client using a dependency injection pattern, rather than a client module building the service.

Applying dependency injection enables us to create a client that does not have any knowledge of the service to be built and of the actual service it is consuming. The client will only have knowledge about the interface of the service as it needs to know how to use the service.

Why dependency injection?

Consider that we are creating a `Mobile` class, and it has dependency on a `camera` and `internet` connectivity.

```
export class Mobile {
  public camera: Camera;
  public internet: Internet;
  constructor() {
    this.camera = new Camera();
    this.internet = new Internet();
  }
  // Method using the camera and internet
  takeSelfieAndShare() {
    return `selfie ` + `${this.camera.photo} shared via internet ${this.internet.type} connectivity.`;
  }
}
```

The code snippet of a Mobile class

In the preceding code snippet, you can see that the instances of `Camera` and `Internet` are created in the constructor of the `Mobile` class. These are the features of Mobile. Instead of requesting for the feature, the `Mobile` class created the feature by itself. This means that the `Mobile` class is bound to a certain version of features, such as a 2 MP camera and 2G Internet. Later, if we want to upgrade the camera to 20 MP and Internet to 3G or 4G, we need to rewrite the code of the `Mobile` class.

The `Mobile` class is dependent on `Camera` and `Internet`, and this increases the difficulty in testing. We can only test Mobile with 2G Internet and 2 MP Camera because we cannot control the dependencies as the `Mobile` class takes care of the instance of dependency by itself.

Now, let's modify the constructor to receive the instance of `Camera` and `Internet` as parameters, as shown in the following line of code:

```
constructor(public camera: Camera, public internet: Internet) { }
```

Now the `Mobile` class will not create an instance of `Camera` or `Internet`. It just consumes the instance of `Camera` or `Internet` that is received from the constructor parameters. This means that we moved the dependencies to the constructor. The client can create a `Mobile` class by passing the instance of `Camera` and `Internet` to the constructor, as shown in the following code snippet:

```
// Simple mobile with 2MP camera and 2G internet.
var mobile = new Mobile(new Camera2MP(), new Internet2G());
```

As you can see, the definitions of `Camera` and `Internet` have been decoupled from the `Mobile` class. We can pass any type of Camera with various megapixels and Internet with various bandwidths, such as 2G, 3G, and 4G, as long as both the `Camera` and `Internet` types passed by the client comply with the interface of `Camera` and `Internet`:

```
// an advanced mobile with 20MP camera and 4G internet.
var mobile = new Mobile(new Camera20MP(), new Internet4G());
```

There is no change in the `Mobile` class to accommodate the 20 MP Camera and 4G Internet dependencies. The `Mobile` class is much easier to test with various combinations of `Camera` and `Internet`, as we have complete control over the dependencies. We can also use a mocking technique in testing and pass mocks of `Camera` and `Internet` to constructor so that all the necessary operations will be done against the mocks of `Camera` and `Internet`.

The role of injectors

We just got to know what a dependency injection is and how it receives dependencies from an external client rather than creating them itself. However, the client needs to update its code to pass an instance of 20 MP Camera and 4G Internet dependencies. Any client that wants to consume the `Mobile` class must create instances of `Camera` and `Internet` as the `Mobile` class depends on them. We eliminated the responsibility for creating the instances of dependencies from the `Mobile` class and moved them to clients that will consume the `Mobile` class.

Now, it has become the poor client's problem to create the instances of `Camera` and `Internet`. So, to reduce the extra efforts of a client in creating the instances of dependencies, we need injectors that take care of assembling instances of the required `Camera` and `Internet` for the client. The dependency injection framework has something called an injector where we register our classes, such as `Mobile`. We can then request the injector to create the instance of `Mobile` for us. The injector will then take care of resolving the dependencies and creating `mobile`, as shown in the following line of code:

```
var mobile = injector.get(Mobile);
```

Handling dependency injection in Angular

Angular has its own dependency injection framework, and we will see, with an example, how it handles dependency injection.

First, we will create a `Todo` class under `app/todos/todo.ts` with properties such as `id`, `description`, and `isCompleted`, as given in the following screenshot:

```
export class Todo {
  id: number;
  description: string;
  isCompleted = false;
}
```

A code snippet of the Todo class

Then, create a `TodoListComponent` component and add the property to hold the collection of todo items retrieved from the injected `TodoService`. The service will be injected into constructor when `TodoListComponent` is instantiated by the dependency injection framework. You will learn more about services in r 3, *Angular Building Blocks - Part 2*.

```typescript
todo-list.component.ts  app
    import { Component }   from '@angular/core';
    import { Todo }        from './todo';
    import { TodoService } from './todo.service';
    @Component({
      selector: 'todo-list',
      template: `
      <div *ngFor="let todo of todos">
        {{todo.id}} - {{todo.description}} <input type="checkbox" [checked]="todo.isCompleted" />
      </div>
      `,
    })
    export class TodoListComponent {
      todos: Todo[];
      constructor(todoService: TodoService) {
        this.todos = todoService.getTodos();
      }
    }
```

A code snippet of the TodoListComponent class

The code is written using Typescript, and when it compiles the code to JavaScript, it includes information about the class metadata, as the class was decorated with `@component`. This class metadata holds the information about associating the `todoService` parameter with the `TodoService` class. This enables the Angular injector to inject the instance of `TodoService` when it creates a new `TodoListComponent`.

We don't explicitly call an injector to inject the service in our code. Instead, Angular's automated dependency injection takes care of it. The injector will be called implicitly while Angular instantiates components when it encounters the `<todo-list>` selector through HTML markups or when navigating to a component via a router.

Now, we will create `TodosComponent`, which registers `TodoService` using the providers parameter in the `@Component` directive. The instance of `TodoService` is readily available for the injection both in `TodosComponent` and in all its child s.

```typescript
import { Component } from '@angular/core';
import { TodoListComponent } from './todo-list.component';
@Component({
  selector: 'my-todos',
```

```
  template: '<h2>Todolist</h2><todo-list></todo-list>',
  providers: [TodoService],
  directives: [TodoListComponent]
})
export class TodosComponent { }
```

Now, let's create the `TodoService` service that returns the collection of todo items.

```
import {TODOS} from './mock-todos'
export class TodoService {
    getTodos() { return TODOS;  }
}
```

The code snippet of TodoService

In the production `TodoList` application, the `getTodos` method in `TodoService` will make an HTTP request to get the list of todos. For the basics, we are returning the collection of todos from the `mock-todos`.

Finally, we need to create `mock-todos`, which holds the collection of todo items, as illustrated in the following screenshot:

```
import { Todo } from './todo';
export var TODOS: Todo[] = [
  { "id": 1, "description": "Jogging", isCompleted: false },
  { "id": 2, "description": "Bathing", isCompleted: false },
  { "id": 3, "description": "Writing", isCompleted: true },
];
```

A code snippet of mock-todos

This file is used as an in-memory collection to hold the todo items, and it is made available to the components that import this file. This approach is good for the development phase, but this needs to be changed in the production phase to fetch todo items from the remote server.

Run the application by pressing *F5* in VS Code, and you will get the output of the Angular TodoList application, as shown in the following screenshot:

The TodoList application running in a browser

Summary

Wow! You must have learned a lot about Angular architecture's core building blocks by now. We started with e and discussed how it encapsulates the functionalities that are independent and have one responsibility. Then, you learned about the concepts of components and how they replaced controllers, scopes, and directives from AngularJS. You also learned about decorators and metadata that leverage the Typescript syntax to make a plain JavaScript class into an Angular component. Then, we discussed templates and the differences between inline templates and isolated templates. You also learned how to implement various binding techniques in a template. Later, we went through directives and how a directive is differentiated from a component. Finally, you learned about one of the most popular design patterns, dependency injection, and how it is handled by Angular.

In the next chapter, we will discuss the remaining blocks in the Angular architecture.

3
Angular Building Blocks - Part 2

This chapter gives you a detailed walk-through on the remaining uncovered core building blocks of the Angular architecture. In this chapter, we will cover the following topics:

- Forms
- Pipes
- Router
- Services
- Observables

Forms

Every application has a data entry point where it enables end users to input data. Forms are meant to insert or update input data to a server and on a page. Input data should be validated before it is submitted for further action. There are two types of validation methods applied: client-side validation and server-side validation:

- **Server-side validation**: Server-side validations will be handled by the server. The information received will be processed and validated by the server. It is necessary to update the UI with appropriate information if there are any errors in submitting the form. If the information is invalid or not sufficient, then the appropriate response will be sent back to the client. This approach to validation is more secure as it works even if JavaScript is turned off in the browser and also, malicious users can't bypass the server-side validation. However, the drawback of this approach is that the form will be validated only after submitting it to the server. So, the user has to wait until the form is fully submitted to the server in order to know whether all the data supplied is valid.

- **Client-side validation**: Though server-side validation is more secure, it will not provide a better user experience. Client-side validations are implemented using a scripting language such as JavaScript, and the validations will be done on the client itself. The user input data can be validated as and when keyed in by the user. This leads to a richer experience by providing immediate response with validation errors on the screen. The user need not wait for the entire form to be submitted to know whether the data entered is valid.

Angular has classes such as FormBuilder, Control, and Validators to handle forms. It enables you to easily set validation rules using Control and Validators.

Tools for forms

Angular has various tools to achieve the preceding scenarios to implement forms in our application. The following are such tools and their respective purposes:

- **Controls**: These provide objects by encapsulating the inputs of forms
- **Validators**: These help in validating the input data from forms
- **Observers**: These help keep track of changes in forms and informs the user of any validation errors

Types of Angular forms

Angular provides two approaches for handling forms: template-driven forms and model-driven forms.

Templete driven forms

AngularJS handled forms using the `ng-model` directive, and it leveraged the power of two-way binding that made the lives of developers easier. Angular enables developers to build template-driven forms using `ngModel`, which is similar to `ng-model` in AngularJS.

The following is the implementation of template-driven forms:

1. Let's create an app named First Template Form in **Visual Studio Code** (**VS Code**).

2. Add the required packages and dependency details in `package.json`, and install them using the `npm` install command.

```
{
"name":"first-template-form",
"version":"1.0.0",
"private":true,
"description":"First template form",
"scripts":{
"test:once":"karma start karma.conf.js --single-
 run",
"build":"tsc -p src/",
"serve":"lite-server -c=bs-config.json",
"prestart":"npm run build",
"start":"concurrently \"npm run build:watch\" \"npm
 run serve\"",
"pretest":"npm run build",
"test":"concurrently \"npm run build:watch\" \"karma
 start
karma.conf.js\"",
"pretest:once":"npm run build",
"build:watch":"tsc -p src/ -w",
"build:upgrade":"tsc",
"serve:upgrade":"http-server",
"build:aot":"ngc -p tsconfig-aot.json && rollup -c
 rollup-
config.js",
"serve:aot":"lite-server -c bs-config.aot.json",
"build:babel":"babel src -d src --extensions
\".es6\" --source-
maps",
"copy-dist-files":"node ./copy-dist-files.js",
"i18n":"ng-xi18n",
"lint":"tslint ./src/**/*.ts -t verbose"
},
"keywords":[
],
"author":"",
"license":"MIT",
"dependencies":{
"@angular/common":"~4.0.0",
"@angular/compiler":"~4.0.0",
"@angular/compiler-cli":"~4.0.0",
"@angular/core":"~4.0.0",
"@angular/forms":"~4.0.0",
"@angular/http":"~4.0.0",
"@angular/platform-browser":"~4.0.0",
```

```
"@angular/platform-browser-dynamic":"~4.0.0",
"@angular/platform-server":"~4.0.0",
"@angular/router":"~4.0.0",
"@angular/tsc-wrapped":"~4.0.0",
"@angular/upgrade":"~4.0.0",
"angular-in-memory-web-api":"~0.3.1",
"core-js":"^2.4.1",
"rxjs":"5.0.1",
"systemjs":"0.19.39",
"zone.js":"^0.8.4"
},
"devDependencies":{
"@types/angular":"^1.5.16",
"@types/angular-animate":"^1.5.5",
"@types/angular-cookies":"^1.4.2",
"@types/angular-mocks":"^1.5.5",
"@types/angular-resource":"^1.5.6",
"@types/angular-route":"^1.3.2",
"@types/angular-sanitize":"^1.3.3",
"@types/jasmine":"2.5.36",
"@types/node":"^6.0.45",
"babel-cli":"^6.16.0",
"babel-preset-angular2":"^0.0.2",
"babel-preset-es2015":"^6.16.0",
"canonical-path":"0.0.2",
"concurrently":"^3.0.0",
"http-server":"^0.9.0",
"jasmine":"~2.4.1",
"jasmine-core":"~2.4.1",
"karma":"^1.3.0",
"karma-chrome-launcher":"^2.0.0",
"karma-cli":"^1.0.1",
"karma-jasmine":"^1.0.2",
"karma-jasmine-html-reporter":"^0.2.2",
"karma-phantomjs-launcher":"^1.0.2",
"lite-server":"^2.2.2",
"lodash":"^4.16.2",
"phantomjs-prebuilt":"^2.1.7",
"protractor":"~4.0.14",
"rollup":"^0.41.6",
"rollup-plugin-commonjs":"^8.0.2",
"rollup-plugin-node-resolve":"2.0.0",
"rollup-plugin-uglify":"^1.0.1",
"source-map-explorer":"^1.3.2",
"tslint":"^3.15.1",
"typescript":"~2.2.0"
},
"repository":{
```

```
}
}
```

3. Create a class book and add the following code snippet:

```
export class Book {
constructor(
public id: number,
public name: string,
public author: string,
public publication?: string
) { }
}
```

4. Create `AppComponent` and add the following code:

```
import { Component } from '@angular/core';
@Component({
selector: 'first-template-form',
template: '<book-form></book-form>'
})
export class AppComponent { }
```

This `AppComponent` shown earlier is the root component of the application that will host the `BookFormComponent`. `AppComponent` is decorated with the first-template-form selector and template that has the inline HTML with the `<book-form/>` special tag. This tag will be updated with the actual template during runtime.

5. Now, let's add the book-form.component.ts with the following code snippet:

```
import { Component } from '@angular/core';
import { Book } from './book';
@Component({selector: 'book-form',
templateUrl: './book-form.component.html'
})
export class BookFormComponent {
model = new Book(1, 'book name','author
name','publication name
is optional');
onSubmit() {
// code to post the data
}
newBook() {
this.model = new Book(0,'','','');
}
}
```

Here, note that we have imported Book from `book.ts`. Book is the data model for this form. `BookFormComponent` is decorated with the `@Component` directive that was imported from `@angular/core`. Selector value is set to `book-form` and the templateUrl is assigned with the template HTML file. In the `BookFormCompoent`, we have instantiated Book model with the dummy data. We have two methods--`onSubmit()` and `newBook()`--one to post the data submitted to API and the other to clear the form.

6. Now, let's add the `book-form.component.html` template file to the following HTML content:

```html
<div class="container">
<h1>New Book Form</h1>
<form (ngSubmit)="onSubmit()" #bookForm="ngForm">
<div class="form-group">
<label for="name">Name</label>
<input type="text" class="form-control" id="name"
required
[(ngModel)]="model.name" name="name"
#name="ngModel">
<div [hidden]="name.valid || name.pristine"
class="alert alert-danger">
Name is required
</div>
</div>
<div class="form-group">
<label for="author">Author</label>
<input type="text" class="form-control" id="author"
required
[(ngModel)]="model.author" name="author"
#author="ngModel">
<div [hidden]="author.valid || author.pristine"
class="alert alert-danger">
Author is required
</div>
</div>
<div class="form-group">
<label for="publication">Publication</label>
<input type="text" class="form-control"
id="publication"
[(ngModel)]="model.publication" name="publication"
#publication="ngModel">
</div>
<button type="submit" class="btn btn-success"
[disabled]="!bookForm.form.valid">Submit</button>
  
<button type="button" class="btn btn-default"
```

```
(click)="newBook()">Clear</button>
</form>
</div>
<style>
.no-style .ng-valid {
border-left: 1px solid #CCC
}
.no-style .ng-invalid {
border-left: 1px solid #CCC
}
</style>
```

This is a simple template form that has three input controls to key in the book, author, and publisher name, a submit button to submit the details, and a Clear button to clear the form. Angular implicitly applies the ngForm directive to the forms in the template. We assigned the ngForm directive to the #bookForm local variable.

Using the #bookForm local variable, we can track the form for errors and check whether they are valid or invalid, touched or untouched, and pristine or dirty. Here, the submit button will be enabled only if the valid property of ngForm returns true, as it is assigned to the button's disabled property.

The onSubmit function from BookFormComponent is assigned to the ngSubmit event of the form. So, when the submit button is clicked on, it will call the onSubmit function in BookFormComponent.

Note that all the input controls contain the ngModel event-cum-property attribute, and it is assigned with their respective model properties, such as model.name, model.author, and model.publication respectively. In this way, we can achieve the two-way binding so that the model properties in BookFormComponent will be updated with their respective values when they are keyed into the corresponding input controls:

1. We have the required template and components in place. Now we need to create an AppModule to bootstrap the root component of our application, AppComponent. Create a file named app.module.ts and add the following code snippet:

```
import { NgModule } from '@angular/core';
import { BrowserModule } from '@angular/platform-
browser';
import { FormsModule } from '@angular/forms';
import { AppComponent } from './app.component';
import { BookFormComponent } from './book-
form.component';
@NgModule({
```

```
    imports: [
    BrowserModule,
    FormsModule
    ],
    declarations: [
    AppComponent,
    BookFormComponent
    ],
    bootstrap: [ AppComponent ]
})
export class AppModule { }
```

As we discussed in `chapter 2` *Angular Building Blocks - Part 1*, any Angular application will have a root module that will be decorated with the `NgModule` directive along with the metadata details, such as imports, declarations, and bootstrap.

In the preceding code, note that we assigned the `AppComponent` class to bootstrap metadata to inform Angular that `AppComponent` is the root component of the application.

2. Now that we have all the required templates and classes in place, we need to bootstrap the module. Let's create a file named `main.ts` with the following code snippet that bootstraps the module:

```
import { platformBrowserDynamic } from
'@angular/platform-
browser-dynamic';
import { AppModule } from './app/app.module';
platformBrowserDynamic().bootstrapModule(AppModule)
```

3. Finally, add the index.html file with the following content:

```
<!DOCTYPE html>
<html>
<head>
<title>Book Form</title>
<base href="/">
<meta charset="UTF-8">
<meta name="viewport" content="width=device-width,
initial-
scale=1">
<link rel="stylesheet"
href="https://unpkg.com/bootstrap@3.3.7/
dist/css/bootstra p.min.cs
s">
<link rel="stylesheet" href="styles.css">
<link rel="stylesheet" href="forms.css">
<!-- Polyfills -->
```

```
<script src="node_modules/core-
js/client/shim.min.js"></script>
<script src="node_modules/zone.js/dist/zone.js">
</script>
<script
src="node_modules/systemjs/dist/system.src.js">
</script>
<script src="systemjs.config.js"></script>
<script>
System.import('main.js').catch(function(err){
console.error(err);
});
</script>
</head>
<body>
<first-template-form>Loading...</first-template-
form>
</body>
</html>
```

Note that the `<first-template-form/>` special tag is added in the body. This tag will be updated with the actual template during runtime. Also, note that the required libraries are loaded during runtime using the `System.js` module loader. The `systemjs.config.js` file should have the instructions on mapping the npm packages and our application's starting point. Here, our application is bootstrapped in the `main.ts`, which will be transpiled to `main.js` after the application is built. The content of the `systemjs.config.js` is given as follows:

```
/**
 * System configuration for Angular samples
 * Adjust as necessary for your application needs.
 */
(function (global) {
System.config({
paths: {
  // paths serve as alias
  'npm:': 'node_modules/'
},
// map tells the System loader where to look for things
map: {// our app is within the app folder
'app': 'app',
// angular bundles
'@angular/animations': 'npm:@angular/animations/bundles/animations.umd.js',
'@angular/animations/browser': 'npm:@angular/animations/bundles/animations-
browser.umd.js',
'@angular/core': 'npm:@angular/core/bundles/core.umd.js',
'@angular/common': 'npm:@angular/common/bundles/common.umd.js',
```

```
'@angular/compiler': 'npm:@angular/compiler/bundles/compiler.umd.js',
'@angular/platform-browser': 'npm:@angular/platform-
browser/bundles/platform-browser.umd.js',
'@angular/platform-browser/animations': 'npm:@angular/platform-
browser/bundles/platform-browser-animations.umd.js',
'@angular/platform-browser-dynamic': 'npm:@angular/platform-browser-
dynamic/bundles/platform-browser-dynamic.umd.js',
'@angular/http': 'npm:@angular/http/bundles/http.umd.js',
'@angular/router': 'npm:@angular/router/bundles/router.umd.js',
'@angular/router/upgrade': 'npm:@angular/router/bundles/router-
upgrade.umd.js',
'@angular/forms': 'npm:@angular/forms/bundles/forms.umd.js',
'@angular/upgrade': 'npm:@angular/upgrade/bundles/upgrade.umd.js',
'@angular/upgrade/static': 'npm:@angular/upgrade/bundles/upgrade-
static.umd.js',
// other libraries
'rxjs': 'npm:rxjs',
'angular-in-memory-web-api': 'npm:angular-in-memory-web-api/bundles/in-
memory-web-api.umd.js'
},
// packages tells the System loader how to load when no filename and/or no
extension
packages: {
app: {
  main: './main.js',
  defaultExtension: 'js',
meta: {
'./*.js': {
  loader: 'systemjs-angular-loader.js'
}
}
},
rxjs: {
  defaultExtension: 'js'
}
}
});
})(this);
```

4. Now, we have all that we need. Let's run the application by pressing *F5*, and the index page will be rendered with the template powered by `BookFormComponent`, as follows:

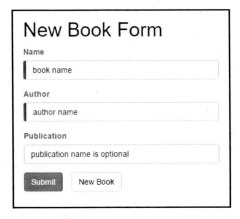

The output of the FIrstTemplateForm application

5. Now remove the dummy texts assigned to input controls and note that the form validation got fired showing the validation error message keeping the **Submit** button in a disabled state:

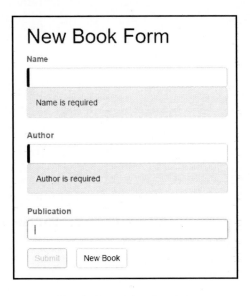

Inspecting the console log to form submit

In this template-drive form, you would have noted that we have applied the required attribute to the input controls. Similar to this, we can also apply minimum length and maximum length validations. However, applying validations like these tightly couples the validation logic to the template, and we can only test these validations by writing browser-based, end-to-end tests.

Model-driven forms

Angular provides the `FormGroup` and `FormControl` attributes to implement model-driven forms.

Fundamental objects of model-driven forms

`FormControl` and `FormGroup` are the two fundamental objects in a model-driven form. `FormControl` is an input field in the Angular form that encapsulates the value of the input field, its state (is valid), if it has changed (is dirty), or has any errors.

When we build a form, we need to create controls and attach metadata to the controls. We have to attach the Control class to the DOM input element by adding the `formControlName` attribute, as shown:

```
<input type="text" formControlName="name" />
```

`FormGroup` can be instantiated by FormBuilder. We can also manually construct `FormGroup` in the components with the default values, as illustrated:

```
this.bookForm = new FormGroup({
  name: new FormControl('book name', Validators.required),
  author: new FormControl('author name', Validators.required),
  publication: new FormControl('publication name is optional')
});
```

Let's create an app named `ModelDrivenForm` in **Visual Studio Code** (**VS Code**). The following is the implementation of model-driven forms:

1. Add the required package and dependency details, and install them using the npm install command:

```
{
"name":"model-driven-form",
"version":"1.0.0",
"private":true,
"description":"Model driven form",
"scripts":{
```

```
"test:once":"karma start karma.conf.js --single-
run",
"build":"tsc -p src/",
"serve":"lite-server -c=bs-config.json",
"prestart":"npm run build",
"start":"concurrently \"npm run build:watch\" \"npm
run serve\"",
"pretest":"npm run build",
"test":"concurrently \"npm run build:watch\" \"karma
start
karma.conf.js\"",
"pretest:once":"npm run build",
"build:watch":"tsc -p src/ -w",
"build:upgrade":"tsc",
"serve:upgrade":"http-server",
"build:aot":"ngc -p tsconfig-aot.json && rollup -c
rollup-
config.js",
"serve:aot":"lite-server -c bs-config.aot.json",
"build:babel":"babel src -d src --extensions
\".es6\" --source-
maps",
"copy-dist-files":"node ./copy-dist-files.js",
"i18n":"ng-xi18n",
"lint":"tslint ./src/**/*.ts -t verbose"
},
"keywords":[
],
"author":"",
"license":"MIT",
"dependencies":{
"@angular/common":"~4.0.0",
"@angular/compiler":"~4.0.0",
"@angular/compiler-cli":"~4.0.0",
"@angular/core":"~4.0.0",
"@angular/forms":"~4.0.0","@angular/http":"~4.0.0",
"@angular/platform-browser":"~4.0.0",
"@angular/platform-browser-dynamic":"~4.0.0",
"@angular/platform-server":"~4.0.0",
"@angular/router":"~4.0.0",
"@angular/tsc-wrapped":"~4.0.0",
"@angular/upgrade":"~4.0.0
",
"angular-in-memory-web-api":"~0.3.1",
"core-js":"^2.4.1",
"rxjs":"5.0.1",
"systemjs":"0.19.39",
"zone.js":"^0.8.4"
```

```
  },
  "devDependencies":{
  "@types/angular":"^1.5.16",
  "@types/angular-animate":"^1.5.5",
  "@types/angular-cookies":"^1.4.2",
  "@types/angular-mocks":"^1.5.5",
  "@types/angular-resource":"^1.5.6",
  "@types/angular-route":"^1.3.2",
  "@types/angular-sanitize":"^1.3.3",
  "@types/jasmine":"2.5.36",
  "@types/node":"^6.0.45",
  "babel-cli":"^6.16.0",
  "babel-preset-angular2":"^0.0.2",
  "babel-preset-es2015":"^6.16.0",
  "canonical-path":"0.0.2",
  "concurrently":"^3.0.0",
  "http-server":"^0.9.0",
  "jasmine":"~2.4.1",
  "jasmine-core":"~2.4.1",
  "karma":"^1.3.0",
  "karma-chrome-launcher":"^2.0.0",
  "karma-cli":"^1.0.1",
  "karma-jasmine":"^1.0.2",
  "karma-jasmine-html-reporter":"^0.2.2",
  "karma-phantomjs-launcher":"^1.0.2",
  "lite-server":"^2.2.2",
  "lodash":"^4.16.2",
  "phantomjs-prebuilt":"^2.1.7",
  "protractor":"~4.0.14",
  "rollup":"^0.41.6",
  "rollup-plugin-commonjs":"^8.0.2",
  "rollup-plugin-node-resolve":"2.0.0",
  "rollup-plugin-uglify":"^1.0.1",
  "source-map-explorer":"^1.3.2",
  "tslint":"^3.15.1",
  "typescript":"~2.2.0"
  },
  "repository":{
  }
  }
```

2. Create a `Book` class and add the following code snippet:

```
export class Book {
constructor(
public id: number,
public name: string,
public author: string,
public publication?: string
) { }
}
```

3. Create `AppComponent` and add the following code:

```
import { Component } from '@angular/core';
@Component({
selector: 'first-model-form',
template: '<book-form></book-form>'
})
export class AppComponent { }
```

This `AppComponent` shown earlier is the root component of the application that will host the `BookFormComponent`. `AppComponent` is decorated with the first-model-form selector and template that has the inline HTML with the `<book-form/>` special tag. This tag will be updated with the actual template during runtime.

4. Now, let's add the `book-form.component.ts` with the following code snippet:

```
import { Component, OnInit } from '@angular/core';
import { FormControl, FormGroup, Validators } from
'@angular/forms';
import { Book } from './book';
@Component({
selector: 'book-form',
templateUrl: './book-form.component.html'
})
export class BookFormComponent implements OnInit {
bookForm: FormGroup;
public submitted: boolean;
constructor() { }
ngOnInit() {
this.bookForm = new FormGroup({
name: new FormControl('book name',
Validators.required),
author: new FormControl('author name',
Validators.required),
publication: new FormControl('publication name is
optional')
```

```
});
}
onSubmit(model: Book, isValid: boolean) {
this.submitted = true;
console.log(model, isValid);
// code to post the data
}
}
```

Here, note that we have imported `FormControl`, `FormGroup`, and `Validators` from `@angular/forms`. These are the essential classes to implement a model-driven form. We have also imported `Component` and `OnInit` from `@angular/core` for Component class implementation, and then we have imported Book from `book.ts`. Book is the data model for this form.

`BookFormComponent` is decorated with the `@Component` directive that was imported from `@angular/core`. Selector value is set to `book-form`, and the `templateUrl` is assigned with the template HTML file.

In the `BookFormCompoent`, we have initialized the form model by instantiating `FormGroup` with the `FormControl` properties instantiated and assigned to properties such as name, author, and publication. We have the `onSubmit()` methods to post the data submitted to API.

5. Now, let's add the `book-form.component.html` template file to the following HTML content:

```
<div class="container">
<h1>New Book Form</h1>
<form [formGroup]="bookForm" novalidate
(ngSubmit)="onSubmit(bookForm.value,
 bookForm.valid)">
<div class="form-group">
<label for="name">Name</label>
<input type="text" class="form-control"
 formControlName="name">
<small [hidden]="bookForm.controls.name.valid ||
(bookForm.controls.name.pristine && !submitted)"
class="text-
danger">
Name is required.
</small>
</div>
<div class="form-group">
<label for="author">Author</label>
<input type="text" class="form-control"
```

```
formControlName="author">
<small [hidden]="bookForm.controls.author.valid ||
(bookForm.controls.author.pristine && !submitted)"
class="text-
danger">
Author is required.
</small>
</div>
<div class="form-group">
<label for="publication">Publication</label>
<input type="text" class="form-control"
formControlName="publication">
</div>
<button type="submit" class="btn btn-
success">Submit</button>
</form>
</div>
<style>
.no-style .ng-valid {
border-left: 1px solid #CCC
}
.no-style .ng-invalid {
border-left: 1px solid #CCC
}
</style>
```

Similar to the template-driven form, this is a simple form based on model driven that has three input controls to key in the book, author, and publisher name and a submit button to submit the details. In the form tag, we have added the `formGroup` directive to the forms and assigned `bookForm` to it. Each input control has a special attribute form `ControlName` assigned with their respective `formControl`, such as name, author, and publication respectively.

The `onSubmit` function from `BookFormComponent` is assigned to the `ngSubmit` event of the form. So, when the submit button is clicked on, it will call the `onSubmit` function in `BookFormComponent`, passing value and valid property of `bookForm`.

Note that all the input controls do not have any event-cum-property attribute as in the template-driven form. Here, we can achieve the two-way binding by passing the model value from the `bookForm.value` property to the `onSubmit` function and accessing the model from component.

We have the required template and components in place. Now we need to create an `AppModule` to bootstrap the root component of our application, `AppComponent`. Create a file named `app.module.ts` and add the following code snippet:

```
import { NgModule } from '@angular/core';
import { BrowserModule } from '@angular/platform-
browser';
import { FormsModule, ReactiveFormsModule } from
'@angular/forms';
import { AppComponent } from './app.component';
import { BookFormComponent } from './book-
form.component';
@NgModule({
imports: [
BrowserModule,
ReactiveFormsModule
],
declarations: [
AppComponent,
BookFormComponent
],
bootstrap: [ AppComponent ]
})
export class AppModule { }
```

In the preceding code, note that we have assigned the `AppComponent` class to bootstrap metadata to inform Angular that `AppComponent` is the root component of the application. Also, note that we have imported `FormsModule` and `ReactiveFormsModule` from `@angular/forms`.

7. Now that we have all the required templates and classes in place, we need to bootstrap the module. Let's create a file named `main.ts` with the following code snippet that bootstraps the module:

```
import { platformBrowserDynamic } from
'@angular/platform-
browser-dynamic';
import { AppModule } from './app/app.module';
platformBrowserDynamic().bootstrapModule(AppModule)
```

8. Finally, add the `index.html` file with the following content:

```
<!DOCTYPE html>
<html>
<head>
<title>Hero Form</title>
<base href="/">
<meta charset="UTF-8">
<meta name="viewport" content="width=device-width,
initial-
scale=1">
<link rel="stylesheet"
href="https://unpkg.com/bootstrap@3.3.7
/dist/css/bootstra    p.min.css">
<link rel="stylesheet" href="styles.css">
<link rel="stylesheet" href="forms.css">
<!-- Polyfills -->
<script src="node_modules/core-
js/client/shim.min.js"></script>
<script src="node_modules/zone.js/dist/zone.js">
</script>
<script
src="node_modules/systemjs/dist/system.src.js">
</script>
<script src="systemjs.config.js"></script>
<script>
System.import('main.js').catch(function(err){
console.error(err);
});
</script>
</head>
<body>
<first-model-form>Loading...</first-model-form>
</body>
</html>
```

Note that the `<first-model-form/>` special tag is added in the body. This tag will be updated with the actual template during runtime. Also, note that the required libraries are loaded during runtime using the `System.js` module loader. The `systemjs.config.js` file should have the instructions on mapping the npm packages and our application's starting point. Here, our application is bootstrapped in the `main.ts`, which will be transpiled to `main.js` after the application is built. The content of the `systemjs.config.js` is given here:

```
/**
* System configuration for Angular samples
* Adjust as necessary for your application needs.
```

```
*/
(function (global) {
System.config({
paths: {
// paths serve as alias
'npm:': 'node_modules/'
},
// map tells the System loader where to look for things
map: {
// our app is within the app folder
'app': 'app',
// angular bundles
'@angular/animations': 'npm:@angular/animations/bundles/animations.umd.js',
'@angular/animations/browser': 'npm:@angular/animations/bundles/animations-
browser.umd.js',
'@angular/core': 'npm:@angular/core/bundles/core.umd.js',
'@angular/common': 'npm:@angular/common/bundles/common.umd.js',
'@angular/compiler': 'npm:@angular/compiler/bundles/compiler.umd.js',
'@angular/platform-browser': 'npm:@angular/platform-
browser/bundles/platform-browser.umd.js',
'@angular/platform-browser/animations': 'npm:@angular/platform-
browser/bundles/platform-browser-animations.umd.js',
'@angular/platform-browser-dynamic': 'npm:@angular/platform-browser-
dynamic/bundles/platform-browser-dynamic.umd.js',
'@angular/http': 'npm:@angular/http/bundles/http.umd.js',
'@angular/router': 'npm:@angular/router/bundles/router.umd.js',
'@angular/router/upgrade': 'npm:@angular/router/bundles/router-
upgrade.umd.js',
'@angular/forms': 'npm:@angular/forms/bundles/forms.umd.js',
'@angular/upgrade': 'npm:@angular/upgrade/bundles/upgrade.umd.js',
'@angular/upgrade/static': 'npm:@angular/upgrade/bundles/upgrade-
static.umd.js',
// other libraries
'rxjs': 'npm:rxjs',
'angular-in-memory-web-api': 'npm:angular-in-memory-web-api/bundles/in-
memory-web-api.umd.js'
},
// packages tells the System loader how to load when no filename and/or no
extension
packages: {
app: {
main: './main.js',
defaultExtension: 'js',
meta: {
'./*.js': {
loader: 'systemjs-angular-loader.js'
}
},
```

```
rxjs: {
defaultExtension: 'js'
}
}
});
})(this);
```

9. Now, we have all that we need. Let's run the application by pressing *F5*, and the index page will be rendered with the template powered by `BookFormComponent`, as follows:

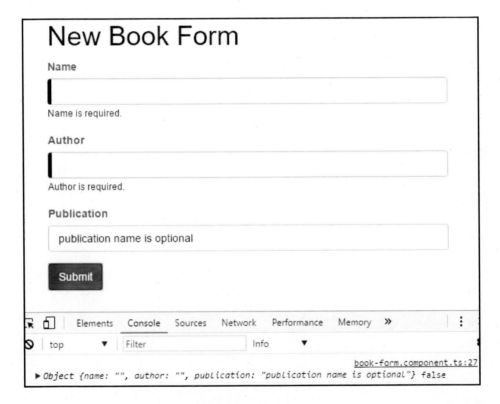

The output of the model-driven form

On clicking on the **Submit** button by keeping the console window open in the developer tools of the Chrome browser, note that the logging model object is logged with the form valid to false as the author property is missing its value.

Now, let's key in some value in the author property and click on the **Submit** button by keeping the console window open in the developer tools of the Chrome browser. Note that the model object logged with the form valid to true will all the required properties filled with value, shown as follows:

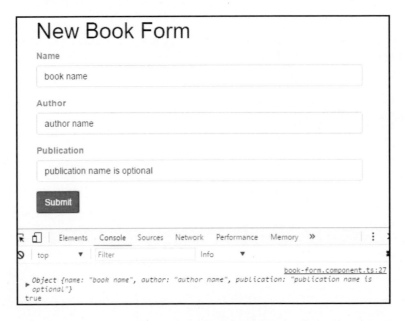

Inspecting the model-driven form submission

As we have configured the validations in the component using `FormGroup`, we have loosely coupled the validation logic by moving it from template to component. So, we can write test methods using any test framework to verify the validation logic by asserting the components. Refer to `Chapter 8`, *Testing Angular applications* to know how to test an angular application.

Pipes

Pipes in Angular are a replacement of filters in AngularJS 1.x. Pipes are an improved version of filters that transform common data. Most of the applications fetch data from a server and transform it before displaying the data on the frontend. In such cases, pipes are very useful in transforming the data on rendering the template. Angular provides these cool API pipes for this purpose. Pipes take data as input and output transformed data as needed.

Common pipes

The following are the built-in pipes available in `@angular/core`, and we will see a few pipes with examples:

- AsyncPipe
- CurrencyPipe
- DatePipe
- DecimalPipe
- I18nPluralPipe
- I18nSelectPipe
- JsonPipe
- LowerCasePipe
- PercentPipe
- SlicePipe
- TitleCasePipe
- UpperCasePipe

Pipe with parameters

We can pass parameters to a pipe followed by a colon (:) symbol, as follows:

```
<p>Price of the book is {{ price | currency:'USD' }} </p>
```

Multiple inputs to a pipe can be added by separating the values by (:), as shown:

```
<li *ngFor="let book of books | slice:1:3">{{i}}</li>
```

Chaining pipes

In some scenarios, it may be necessary to use more than one pipe. For example, consider a scenario to display data in uppercase, long formatted date. The following code displays the publishing date of a book in uppercase and in long formatted date:

```
Publishing Date: {{ pubDate | date | uppercase}}
```

Currency pipes

Currency pipes format the number to the required currency format that is provided. This is the syntax for a currency pipe:

```
expression | currency[:currencyCode[:symbolDisplay[:digitInfo]]]
```

The `expression` is the input data for a pipe; `currency` is the keyword of the pipe, and it takes three arguments, namely `currencyCode`, which takes values such as USD, INR, GBP, and EUR, `symbolDisplay`, which accepts true or false to show/hide the currency symbol, and `digitInfo`, which takes the decimal format for the currency. The following template demonstrates how to use the currency pipe:

```html
<h4>CurrencyPipe</h4>
<p>
    Original Currency Value: {{ currencyData }}<br/>
    US Dollar Format: {{ currencyData | currency: 'USD': true: '.2-2' }}<br/>
    GB Pound Format: {{ currencyData | currency: 'GBP': true: '.2-2' }}<br/>
    Euro Format: {{ currencyData | currency: 'EUR': true: '.2-2' }}
</p>
```

The template that implements a currency pipe

The output of the template will be as follows for various currency formats:

CurrencyPipe

Original Currency Value: 50
US Dollar Format: $50.00
GB Pound Format: £50.00
Euro Format: €50.00

The output of using a currency pipe

Date pipes

Date pipes transform input data to various date formats that are supported by a date pipe. The syntax of the date pipe is as follows:

```
expression | date[:format]
```

Let's assume that `dateData` is assigned with `Date.now()` in a component. The implementation of the date pipe in the template is as shown in the following screenshot:

```
<h4>DatePipe</h4>
<p>
    Original Date Value: {{ dateData }}<br/>
    Default Date Format: {{ dateData | date }}<br/>
    Full Date Format: {{ dateData | date: 'fullDate' }}<br/>
    Only Time: {{ dateData | date: 'jmZ' }}
</p>
```

The template that implements the date pipe

The output of this template after applying various date formats is as follows:

DatePipe

Original Date Value: 1456185983693
Default Date Format: Feb 23, 2016
Full Date Format: Tuesday, February 23, 2016
Only Time: 5:36 AM GMT+5:30

The output of using a date pipe

A date pipe supports various formats, such as `medium` (yMMMdjms), `short` (yMdjm), `mediumDate` (yMMMd), `shortDate` (yMd), `fullDate` (yMMMMEEEEd), `longDate` (yMMMMd), `mediumTime` (jms), and `shortTime` (jm).

Uppercase and lowercase pipes

Uppercase and lowercase pipes transform input data into uppercase and lowercase respectively. The following template displays an author name both in lowercase and uppercase:

```
<h4>UpperCasePipe and LowerCasePipe</h4>
<p>
    Original Value: {{ authorName }}<br/>
    Uppercase Value: {{ authorName | uppercase }}<br/>
    Lowercase Value: {{ authorName | lowercase }}
</p>
```

The template that implements the uppercase and lowercase pipes

The output of this template is as follows:

UpperCasePipe and LowerCasePipe

Original Value: rAjEsH gUnAsUnDaRaM
Uppercase Value: RAJESH GUNASUNDARAM
Lowercase Value: rajesh gunasundaram

The output of implementing an uppercase and lowercase pipe

JSON pipes

A JSON pipe is similar to applying JSON.Stringify in JavaScript to an object that holds JSON values. The usage of a JSON pipe in a template is shown in this screenshot:

```
<h4>JsonPipe</h4>
<p>Without JSON pipe:</p>
<pre>{{object}}</pre>
<p>With JSON pipe:</p>
<pre>{{object | json}}</pre>
```

The template that implements the JSON pipe

The output of using a JSON pipe in a template is as illustrated:

JsonPipe

Without JSON pipe:

[object Object]

With JSON pipe:

```
{
  "autherName": "Rajesh Gunasundaram",
  "pubName": "Packt Publishing"
}
```

The output of using the JSON pipe

AppComponent

`AppComponent` is the component of an application that is configured as root component, and it handles the rendering of the `app.component.html` template. In the preceding sections, we saw the template code that implemented various pipes and their respective output. The following code snippet shows the component for the template:

```
import { Component } from '@angular/core';

@Component({
  selector: 'pipe-page',
  templateUrl: 'app/app.component.html'
})
export class AppComponent {
    numberData : number;
    currencyData : number;
    dateData : number;
    authorName : string;
    object: Object = {autherName: 'Rajesh Gunasundaram',
    pubName: 'Packt Publishing'}
    constructor() {
        this.numberData = 123.456789;
        this.currencyData = 50;
        this.dateData = Date.now();
        this.authorName = 'rAjEsH gUnAsUnDaRaM';
    }
}
```

Pipes, very powerful and simple-to-use APIs provided by Angular, ease our process of formatting data before displaying it on the screen.

Routers

AngularJS used the `ngRoute` module to run simple routers with basic features. It enables deep linking of URLs to components and views by mapping the path to the routes configured using the `$routeProvider` service. AngularJS 1.x needs the `ngRoute` module to be installed to implement routing in an application.

Angular introduced a Component Router that deep links the URL request and navigates to the template or view. It passes parameters, if any, to the respective component that is annotated for this route.

The core concept of Component Routers

Angular uses a Component Router for a view system. It also works on AngularJS 1.x. It supports intercepting routes and providing route-specific values to the loaded component, automatic deep linking, nested, and sibling routes. Let's go through some of the core features of Component Routers.

Setting up a Component Router

A Component Router is not part of the core Angular framework. It comes as part of the Angular NPM bundle as an individual library, @angular/router. We need to add @angular/router to the packages.json under the dependencies section. Then, in the app.routing.ts, we need to import Routes and RouterModule from @angular/router. The router constitutes directives such as RouterOutlet, RouterLink, and RouterLinkActive, a service RouterModule and the configuration for Routes.

Then, we need to add the <base> element under <head> to instruct the router to set up navigation URLs. The following code snippet shows the <base> tag with the href attribute that is to be added to the head tag in the index file, considering that the app folder is the root of the application. This is required when you run your application in HTML5 mode. It helps resolve all the relative URLs in the application:

```
<base href="/">
```

Configuring routes

The routes have information about selecting the view to render when a user clicks on a link for navigation. The following code snippet shows how to configure routes in app.module.ts:

```
import { RouterModule } from '@angular/router';
RouterModule.forRoot([
{
  path: 'about',
  component: AboutComponent
},
{
  path: 'contact',
  component: ContactComponent
}
])
```

Here, we have configured two routes that help the user navigate to the about and contact views when clicked on. Routes are basically a collection of route definitions. The value of the path defined identifies the component to be instantiated when the URL in the browser matches the path. Then, the instantiated component will take care of rendering the view.

Now, we need to add the configured routes to the AppModule, import the RouterModule from @angular/router, and add it to the imports section of @NgModule, as described:

```
import { NgModule } from '@angular/core';
import { BrowserModule } from '@angular/platform-browser';
import { RouterModule } from '@angular/router';
import { AppComponent } from './app.component';
import { AboutComponent } from './heroes.component';
@NgModule({
   imports: [
   BrowserModule,
   FormsModule,
   RouterModule.forRoot([
{
   path: 'about',
   component: AboutComponent
}
])
],
declarations: [
AppComponent,
AboutComponent
],
bootstrap: [ AppComponent ]
})
export class AppModule { }
```

Here, the forRoot() method provides router service providers and directives to perform navigation.

Router Outlet and Router Links

When the user passes '/about' in the address bar of the browser appending to the end of the application URL, the router will match the request with the 'about' and initiate the AboutComponent to handle rendering the view for about. We need to somehow inform the router where to display this about view. This can be achieved by specifying <router-outlet/>, which is similar to the <ng-view/> tag in AngularJS 1.x to load the templates associated with the corresponding path of the route.

Router links help navigate the route URL via the link specified in the anchor tag by clicking on the router link. A sample router link tag is given here:

```
<a [routerLink]="['/about']">About</a>
```

Services

The applications we create handle volumes of data. Most of the data will be retrieved from services and will be reused in various parts of the application. Let's create a service that can retrieve data using `http`. The service should be loosely coupled with components, as the primary focus of the component should be to support the view. So, the service can be injected to components using a dependency injection. This approach will enable us to mock the service in order to unit test the component.

Let's create a simple `TodoService` that returns a list of `Todo` items. The code snippet of `TodoService` is shown here. `TodoService` has a property named `todos` of the type array that can hold a collection of `Todo` items and is hardcoded with the `Todo` items in the constructor:

```
import {Injectable} from '@angular/core';
import { Todo } from './todo';

@Injectable()
export class TodoService {
    todos: Array<Todo>;
    constructor() {
        this.todos = [
    {"title": "First Todo", "completed":  false},
    {"title": "Second Todo", "completed": false},
    {"title": "Third Todo", "completed": false}
            ]
    }
    getTodos() {
        return this.todos;
    }
}
```

Note that the service decorated with `@Injectable` is to let Angular know that this service is injectable.

We can inject the injectable `TodoService` to the constructor of `AppComponent`, as follows:

```
import { Component } from '@angular/core';
import { Todo } from './Todo';
import { TodoService } from './TodoService';
@Component({
  selector: 'my-service',
  templateUrl: 'app/app.component.html'
})
export class AppComponent {
    todos: Array<Todo>;
    constructor(todoService: TodoService) {
        this.todos = todoService.getTodos();
    }
}
```

When bootstrapping, we also need to pass `TodoService` so that Angular will create an instance of the service and keep it available wherever it is injected. So, let's pass `TodoService` to the bootstrap function, as illustrated, in the `main.ts` file:

```
import { NgModule } from '@angular/core';
import { BrowserModule } from '@angular/platform-browser';
import { AppComponent } from './app.component';
import { TodoService } from './TodoService';
@NgModule({
imports: [
BrowserModule,
],
declarations: [
AppComponent,
],
providers: [ TodoService ],
bootstrap: [ AppComponent ]
})
export class AppModule { }
```

Note that the injectable service is wrapped with square brackets. This is one way of applying the dependency injection. Refer to `Chapter 2`, *Angular Building Blocks - Part 1*, for more information on the dependency injection in Angular. Angular has improved dependency injection that takes care of creating an instance of `TodoService` and injecting it to Component.

In the `app.component.html` template, we iterate each item of the `todos` property in `AppComponent` and list them:

```html
<h2>My Todo List</h2>
<ul>
    <li *ngFor="let todo of todos">
        {{ todo.title }} - {{ todo.completed }}
    </li>
</ul>
```

The content of this template will be rendered under the `<my-service>` special tag in the body of the `index.html` file:

```html
<body>
        <my-service>Loading...</my-service>
</body>
```

On running, the application will render the list of `todo` items, as shown:

The output of my to-do application

Observables

In AngularJS, we consumed services to retrieve data asynchronously using promises in `$http`. In Angular, we have the `Http` service over `$http`, and it returns an observable object instead of a promise as it applies a pattern called the analogous pattern. Angular leverages the Observable class adopted from the ReactiveX library. ReactiveX is an API for asynchronous programming with Observables that is done by applying the observer and iterator patterns and functional programming. You can find more information about Reactive programming at `http://reactivex.io/`.

Observer pattern will notify the dependents if their dependency object is changed. Iterator pattern will facilitate access to a collection without the need to know about the structure of the element in the collection. Combining these patterns in ReactiveX enables the observer to subscribe to an observable collection objection. The observer doesn't need to wait until the observable collection object is available. Instead, the observer will react when it gets the notification of the changes in the observables.

Angular uses the JavaScript implementation called RxJS, which is a set of libraries rather than a specific API. It uses Observables in the HTTP service and event system. A promise always returns one value.

The `http.get()` method will return Observables, and this can be subscribed by a client to get the data returned from the service. Observables can handle multiple values. So, we can also call multiple `http.get()` methods and wrap them under the `forkJoin` method that is exposed by Observables.

We can also control the service call and delay the call using Observable by applying a rule to call the service only if the previous call to the service was 500 milliseconds ago.

Observables are cancelable. So, it is also possible to cancel the previous request by unsubscribing to it and making a new request. We can cancel any previously unserved call anytime.

Let's modify `TodoService` to use Observable and replace the hardcoded JSON value with the `http.get()` call to a `todos.json` file. The updated `TodoService` is shown here:

```
import {Injectable} from '@angular/core';
import {Http} from '@angular/http';
import 'rxjs/add/operator/toPromise';
@Injectable()
export class TodoService {
constructor(private http: Http) {
this.http = http;
}
getTodos() {
  return this.http.get('/app/todos.json')
  .toPromise()
  .then(response => response.json().data)
  .catch(this.handleError);
}
}
```

Note that we have imported HTTP modules, response from `@angular/http`, and the Observable module from `rsjs/Rx`, which is based on ReactiveX. The `getTodos` method is updated with an `http.get()` call that queries `todos.json` and returns a collection of to-do items.

`AppComponent` and `TodoService` are bootstrapped in the `app.module.ts` file, as shown:

```
import { NgModule } from '@angular/core';
import { BrowserModule } from '@angular/platform-browser';
import { HttpModule } from '@angular/http';
import { AppComponent } from './app.component';
import { TodoComponent } from './todo.component';
import { TodoService } from './hero.service';
@NgModule({
  imports: [
  BrowserModule,
  HttpModule,
  AppRoutingModule
  ],
  declarations: [
  AppComponent,
  TodoComponent
  ],
  providers: [ TodoService ],
  bootstrap: [ AppComponent ]
})
export class AppModule { }
```

Import `{bootstrap}` from `'@angular/platform-browser-dynamic'`; the template is updated to render the list of todos, as follows:

```
import {HTTP_PROVIDERS} from '@angular/http';
import 'rxjs/add/operator/map';
import {AppComponent} from './app.component';
import {TodoService} from './TodoService';
bootstrap(AppComponent, [HTTP_PROVIDERS, TodoService]);
```

Running the application will render the data subscribed from Observables that is returned by the methods in `TodoService`:

My Service Call using Observables:

My Todos

- First Todo
- Second Todo
- Third Todo

The output of index.html that renders the data subscribed from Observables

Summary

Woohoo! You've completed learning the rest of the building blocks of the Angular architecture. We started the chapter with forms and walked through the types of forms available in Angular and how to implement them. Then, you learned about pipes, which is an alternative to filters in AngularJS 1.x. Next, we discussed routers, and you learned how easy it is to configure a router to a component in Angular. Finally, you learned how to create a service in Angular and how to access an external service using the HTTP module. You also learned about the advantages of using Observables and implementing it in service calls.

In the next chapter, we will discuss the fundamentals of TypeScript.

4

Using TypeScript with Angular

This chapter discusses the fundamentals of TypeScript and the benefits of using TypeScript to write Angular applications.

In this chapter, we will cover the following topics:

- What is TypeScript?
- Basic types
- Interfaces
- Classes
- Modules
- Functions
- Generics
- Decorators
- TypeScript and Angular

What is TypeScript?

TypeScript is an open source programming language developed and maintained by Microsoft. It is a superset of JavaScript, and facilitates writing object-oriented programming. It should be compiled with JavaScript to run on any browser.

TypeScript provides the greatest tooling and advanced autocompletion, navigation, and refactoring. It is used to develop the JavaScript application for the client side and server side. With classes, modules, and interfaces, we can build robust components using TypeScript.

The main advantage it provides over JavaScript is that it enables compile time type checking for errors. Unexpected runtime errors can be avoided due to casting issues. Also, it provides syntactic sugar for writing object-oriented programming.

Basic types

In a programming language, we deal with various small units of data, such as `numbers`, `sting`, and `Boolean` values. TypeScript supports these types of data, as in JavaScript, with enumeration and structure types.

Boolean

The `boolean` data type can hold either `true` or `false`. Declaring and initializing this data type is quite easy and is illustrated as follows:

```
let isSaved: boolean = false;
```

Here, the `isSaved` variable is declared as `boolean` and is assigned with the value `false`. If the developer assigns a string value to the `isSaved` variable by mistake, the TypeScript will show an error and highlight the statement.

Number

The number data type holds floating-point values. Similar to JavaScript, TypeScript considers all numbers as floating-point values. Declaring and initializing the number data type variable can be done as follows:

```
let price: number = 101;
```

Here, the `price` variable is declared as `number` and is assigned the value 101. Number type can hold values such as decimal, binary, hexadecimal, and octal literals, as shown:

```
let decimal: number = 6;
let hex: number = 0xf00d;
let binary: number = 0b1010;
let octal: number = 0o744;
```

String

The string data type can hold a sequence of characters. Declaring and initializing the `string` variable is very simple, as illustrated:

```
let authorName: string = "Rajesh Gunasundaram";
```

Here, we declared a variable named `authorName` as `string`, and assigned it the "Rajesh Gunasundaram" value. TypeScript supports the `string` value surrounded either by double quotes (") or single quotes (').

Array

The array data type is meant to hold the collection of values of specific types. In TypeScript, we can define `array` in two ways, which are as follows:

```
var even:number[] = [2, 4, 6, 8, 10];
```

This statement declares an array variable of the `number` type using square brackets ([]) after the `number` data type, and it is assigned a series of even numbers from 2 to 10. The second way to define array is this:

```
let even:Array<number> = [2, 4, 6, 8, 10];
```

This statement uses the generic array type that uses the `Array` keyword followed by angle brackets (<>) that wrap the `number` data type.

Enum

The enum data type will have a named set of values. We use enumerators to give friendly names to constants that identify certain values:

```
enum Day {Mon, Tue, Wed, Thu, Fri, Sat, Sun};
let firstDay: Day = Day.Mon;
```

Here, we have the `enum` type `Day` variable that holds the series of values representing each day of a week. The second statement shows how to access a particular `enum` value in a day and assign the same to another variable.

Any

The `Any` data type is a dynamic data type that can hold `Any` value. TypeScript throws compile time errors if you assign a string-type variable to an integer-type variable. If you are unsure about what value a variable will hold, and you would like to opt out of compiler checking for the type in the assignment, you can use the `Any` data type:

```
let mixedList:any[] = [1, "I am string", false];
mixedList [2] = "no you are not";
```

Here, we used an array of the any type so that it can hold any type, such as `number`, `string`, and `boolean`.

Void

The void is actually nothing. It can be used as the return type of a function to declare that this function will not return any value:

```
function alertMessage(): void {
    alert("This function does not return any value");
}
```

Interfaces

An interface is an abstract type that defines the behavior of a class. It provides a type definition for an object that can be exchanged between clients. This enables the client to only exchange an object that is compiled with the interface type definition; otherwise, we get a compile time error.

In TypeScript, interfaces define contracts of an object within your code and the code outside your project. Let's see how to use TypeScript with an example:

```
function addCustomer(customerObj: {name: string}) {
  console.log(customerObj.name);
}
let customer = {id: 101, name: "Rajesh Gunasundaram"};
addCustomer(customer);
```

The type-checker verifies the `addCustomer` method call and examines its parameter. The `addCustomer` expects an object with the `name` property of the `string` type. However, the client that calls `addCustomer` passed an object with two parameters: `id` and `name`, respectively.

However, the compiler ignores checking the `id` property as it is not available in the parameter type of the `addCustomer` method. What matters for the compiler is that the required properties are present.

Let's rewrite the method applying `interface` as a parameter type, as demonstrated:

```
interface Customer {
  name: string;
}
function addCustomer(customerObj: Customer) {
  console.log(customerObj.name);
}
let customer = {id: 101, name: "Rajesh Gunasundaram"};
addCustomer(customer);
```

Here, we declared the `Customer` interface with the `name` parameter, and we modified the `addCustomer` signature to accept the parameter of the type `Customer` interface. The remaining statements are the same as the preceding code snippet. The compiler only checks for the shape of the object. It will not check whether the object we are passing implements the `Customer` interface. It only looks for the `name` property of the `string` type in the parameter and then allows it if present.

Optional properties

In some scenarios, we may want to pass values only for minimal parameters. In such cases, we can define the properties in an interface as optional properties, as follows:

```
interface Customer {
  id: number;
  name: string;
  bonus?: number;
}
function addCustomer(customer: Customer) {
  if (customer.bonus) {
    console.log(customer.bonus);
  }
}
addCustomer({id: 101, name: "Rajesh Gunasundaram"});
```

Here, the bonus property has been defined as an optional property by concatenating a question mark (?) at the end of the name property.

Function type interfaces

We just saw how to define properties in interfaces. Similarly, we can also define function types in interfaces. We can define function types in interfaces just by giving the signature of the function with the return type. Note that in the following code snippet, we have not added the function name:

```
interface AddCustomerFunc {
   (firstName: string, lastName: string); void
}
```

Now, AddCustomerFunc is ready. Let's define a function type variable, AddCustomerFunc, and assign a function of the same signature to it as follows:

```
let addCustomer: AddCustomerFunc;
addCustomer = function(firstName: string, lastName: string) {
   console.log('Full Name: ' + firstName + ' ' + lastName);
}
```

The parameter name in the function signature can vary but not the data type. For example, we can alter the fn and ln function parameters of the string type, as follows:

```
addCustomer = function(fn: string, ln: string) {
console.log('Full Name: ' + fn + ' ' + ln);
}
```

So, if we change the data type of the parameter or the return type of the function here, the compiler will throw an error about the parameter not matching or the return type not matching with the AddCustomerFunc interface.

Array type interfaces

We can also define an interface for array types. We can specify the data type for the `index` array and the data type to the array item, as shown:

```
interface CutomerNameArray {
  [index: number]: string;
}
let customerNameList: CutomerNameArray;
customerNameList = ["Rajesh", "Gunasundaram"];
```

TypeScript supports two types of `index`, namely `number`, and `string`. This array type interface also enforces that the return type of the array should match the declaration.

Class type interfaces

Class type interfaces define the contract for classes. A class that implements an interface should meet the requirements of the interface:

```
interface CustomerInterface {
    id: number;
    firstName: string;
    lastName: string;
    addCustomer(firstName: string, lastName: string);
    getCustomer(id: number): Customer;
}
class Customer implements CustomerInterface {
    id: number;
    firstName: string;
    lastName: string;
    constructor() { }
    addCustomer(firstName: string, lastName: string): void {
        // code to add customer
    }
    getCustomer(id: number): Customer {
        // code to return customer where the id match with id parameter
    }
}
```

The class type interface only deals with public members of the class. So, it is not possible to add private members to the interface.

Extending interfaces

Interfaces can be extended; extending an interface makes it share the properties of another interface, as follows:

```
interface Manager {
    hasPower: boolean;
}
interface Employee extends Manager {
    name: string;
}
let employee = <Employee>{};
employee.name = "Rajesh Gunasundaram";
employee.hasPower = true;
```

Here, the `Employee` interface extends the `Manager` interface and shares its `hasPower` with the `Employee` interface.

Hybrid type interface

Hybrid type interfaces are used when we want to use an object both as a function and as an object. We can call an object like a function if it implements a hybrid type interface, or we can use it as an object and access its properties. This type of interface enables you to use an interface as an object and a function, as illustrated:

```
interface Customer {
    (name: string): string;
    name: string;
    deleteCustomer(id: number): void;
}
let c: Customer;
c('Rajesh Gunasundaram');
c.name = 'Rajesh Gunasundaram';
c.deleteCustomer(101);
```

Classes

A class is an extensible template that is used to create objects with member variables to hold the state of the object and member functions that deal with the behavior of the object.

The current version of JavaScript supports only function-based and prototype-based inheritance to build reusable components. The next version of JavaScript ECMAScript 6 supports object-oriented programming by adding the syntactic sugar for prototype-based class definitions and inheritance. However, TypeScript enabled developers to write code using object-oriented programming techniques, and it compiles the code down to JavaScript, which is compatible with all browsers and platforms:

```
class Customer {
    name: string;
    constructor(name: string) {
        this.name = name;
    }
    logCustomer() {
        console.log('customer name is ' + this.name);
    }
}
let customer = new Customer("Rajesh Gunasundaram");
```

This `Customer` class has three members: a `name` property, a constructor, and a `logCustomer` method. The last statement outside the `Customer` class creates an instance of the `customer` class using the `new` keyword.

Inheritance

Inheritance is the concept of inheriting some behaviors of another class or object. It helps achieve code reusability and build hierarchy in relationships of classes or objects. Also, inheritance helps you cast similar classes.

JavaScript of ES5 standard doesn't support classes, and so, class inheritance is not possible in JavaScript. However, we can implement prototype inheritance instead of class inheritance. Let's see inheritance in ES5 with examples.

First, create a function named `Animal`, as follows. Here, we create a function named `Animal` with two methods: `sleep` and `eat`:

```
var Animal = function() {
    this.sleep = function() {
        console.log('sleeping');
    }
    this.eat = function() {
        console.log('eating');
    }
}
```

Now, let's extend this `Animal` function using the prototype, as shown:

```
Animal.prototype.bark = function() {
    console.log('barking');
}
```

Now, we can create an instance of `Animal` and call the extended function bark, as demonstrated:

```
var a = new Animal();
a.bark();
```

We can use the `Object.Create` method to clone a prototype of the parent and create a child object. Then, we can extend the child object by adding methods. Let's create an object named `Dog` and inherit it from `Animal`:

```
var Dog = function() {
    this.bark = new function() {
        console.log('barking');
    }
}
```

Now, let's clone the prototype of `Animal` and inherit all the behavior in the `Dog` function. Then, we can call the `Animal` method using the `Dog` instance, as follows:

```
Dog.prototype = Object.create(animal.prototype);
var d = new Dog();
d.sleep();
d.eat();
```

Inheritance in TypeScript

We just saw how to implement an inheritance in JavaScript using a prototype. Now, we will see how an inheritance can be implemented in TypeScript.

In TypeScript, similar to extending interfaces, we can also extend a class by inheriting another class, as illustrated:

```
class SimpleCalculator {
    z: number;
    constructor() { }
    addition(x: number, y: number) {
        z = x + y;
    }
    subtraction(x: number, y: number) {
        z = x - y;
```

```
        }
    }
    class ComplexCalculator extends SimpleCalculator {
        constructor() { super(); }
        multiplication(x: number, y: number) {
            z = x * y;
        }
        division(x: number, y: number) {
            z = x / y;
        }
    }
    var calculator = new ComplexCalculator();
    calculator.addition(10, 20);
    calculator.Substraction(20, 10);
    calculator.multiplication(10, 20);
    calculator.division(20, 10);
```

Here, we are able to access the methods of `SimpleCalculator` using the instance of `ComplexCalculator` as it extends `SimpleCalculator`.

Private/Public modifiers

In TypeScript, all members in a class are `public` by default. We have to add the `private` keyword explicitly to control the visibility of the members:

```
    class SimpleCalculator {
        private x: number;
        private y: number;
        z: number;
        constructor(x: number, y: number) {
            this.x = x;
            this.y = y;
        }
        addition() {
            z = x + y;
        }
        subtraction() {
            z = x - y;
        }
    }
    class ComplexCalculator {
        z: number;
        constructor(private x: number, private y: number) { }
        multiplication() {
            z = this.x * this.y;
        }
    }
```

```
    division() {
        z = this.x / this.y;
    }
}
```

Note that in the `SimpleCalculator` class, we defined x and y as `private` properties, which will not be visible outside the class. In `ComplexCalculator`, we defined x and y using parameter properties. These parameter properties will enable us to create and initialize the member in one statement. Here, x and y are created and initialized in the constructor itself without writing any further statements inside it. Also, x and y are private in order to hide them from exposure to consuming classes or modules.

Accessors

We can also implement `getters` and `setters` to the properties to control accessing them from the client. We can intercept some process before setting a value to a property variable or before getting a value of the property variable:

```
var updateCustomerNameAllowed = true;
Class Customer {
    Private _name: string;
    get name: string {
        return this._name;
    }
    set name(newName: string) {
        if (updateCustomerNameAllowed == true) {
            this._name = newName;
        }
        else {
            alert("Error: Updating Customer name not allowed!");
        }
    }
}
```

Here, the `setter` for the name property ensures that the customer name can be updated. Otherwise, it will show an alert message that it is not possible.

Static properties

These type of properties are not instance specific and are accessed by a class name instead of using the `this` keyword:

```
class Customer {
    static bonusPercentage = 20;
    constructor(public salary: number) {  }
     calculateBonus() {
         return this.salary * Customer.bonusPercentage/100;
    }
}
var customer = new Customer(10000);
var bonus = customer.calculateBonus();
```

Here, we declared a `static` variable, `bonusPercentage`, accessed using the `Customer` class name in the `calculateBonus` method. The `bonusPercentage` property is not instance specific.

Modules

JavaScript is a powerful and dynamic language. Due to the liberty of dynamic programming in JavaScript as per ES5 and earlier standards, it is our duty to structure and organize code. It will make the maintainability of code easier and also enable us to easily locate the code of a specific functionality we need. We can organize code by applying a modular pattern. Code can be separated into various modules, and the relevant code can be put in each module.

TypeScript made it easier to implement modular programming using the keyword module as per ECMAScript 6 specifications. Modules enable you to control the scope of variables, code reusability, and encapsulation. TypeScript supports two types of modules: internal and external.

Namespaces

We can create namespaces in TypeScript using the namespace keyword, as illustrated. All the classes defined under namespace will be scoped under that particular namespace and will not be attached to the global scope:

```
namespace Inventory {
    Class Product {
            constructor (public name: string, public quantity: number) {
```

```
}
        }
        // product is accessible
        var p = new Product('mobile', 101);
}
// Product class is not accessible outside namespace
var p = new Inventory.Product('mobile', 101);
```

To make the `Product` class available outside the namespace, we need to add an `export` keyword when defining the `Product` class, as follows:

```
namespace Inventory {
        export Class Product {
                constructor (public name: string, public quantity: number) {
}
        }
}
// Product class is now accessible outside Inventory namespace
var p = new Inventory.Product('mobile', 101);
```

We can also share the namespace across files by adding a `reference` statement at the beginning of the code in the referring files, as shown:

```
/// <reference path="Inventory.ts" />
```

Modules

TypeScript also supports modules. As we deal with a large number of external JavaScript libraries, this module will really help us refer and organize our code. Using the `import` statement, we can import external modules, as illustrated:

```
Import { inv } from "./Inventory";
var p = new inv.Product('mobile', 101);
```

Here, we just imported the previously created module, `Inventory`, and created an instance of `Product` assigned to the p variable.

Functions

JavaScript that follows ES5 specificaitons does not support classes and modules. However, we tried to achieve the scoping of variables and modularity using functional programming in JavaScript. Functions are the building blocks of an application in JavaScript.

Though TypeScript supports classes and modules, functions play a key role in defining a specific logic. We can define both the `function` and `Anonymous` functions in JavaScript as shown:

```
//Named function
function multiply(a, b) {
    return a * b;
}
//Anonymous function
var result = function(a, b) { return a * b; };
```

In TypeScript, we define functions with the type of the parameters and the return type using function arrow notation, which is also supported in ES6; it's done like this:

```
var multiply(a: number, b: number) => number =
         function(a: number, b: number): number { return a * b; };
```

Optional and default parameters

Consider that we have a function with three parameters, and sometimes, we may only pass values for the first two parameters in the function. In TypeScript, we can handle such scenarios using the optional parameter. We can define the first two parameters as normal and the third parameter as optional, as given in the following code snippet:

```
function CutomerName(firstName: string, lastName: string, middleName?:
string) {
    if (middleName)
        return firstName + " " + middleName + " " + lastName;
    else
        return firstName + " " + lastName;
}
//ignored optional parameter middleName
var customer1 = customerName("Rajesh", "Gunasundaram");
//error, supplied too many parameters
var customer2 = customerName("Scott", "Tiger", "Lion", "King");
//supplied values for all
var customer3 = customerName("Scott", "Tiger", "Lion");
```

Here, `middleName` is the optional parameter, and it can be ignored when calling the function.

Now, let's see how to set default parameters in a function. If a value is not supplied to a parameter in the `function`, we can define it to take the default value that is configured:

```
function CutomerName(firstName: string, lastName: string, middleName:
string = 'No Middle Name') {
    if (middleName)
        return firstName + " " + middleName + " " + lastName;
    else
        return firstName + " " + lastName;
}
```

Here, `middleName` is the default parameter that will have `'No Middle Name'` by default if the value is not supplied by the caller.

Rest parameters

Using the rest parameter, you can pass an array of values to the function. This can be used in scenarios where you are unsure about how many values will be supplied to the function:

```
function clientName(firstClient: string, ...restOfClient: string[]) {
    console.log(firstClient + " " + restOfClient.join(" "));
}
clientName ("Scott", "Steve", "Bill", "Sergey", "Larry");
```

Here, note that the `restOfClient` rest parameter is prefixed with an ellipsis (...), and it can hold an array of strings. In the caller of the function, only the value of the first parameter that is supplied will be assigned to the `firstClient` parameter, and the remaining values will be assigned to `restOfClient` as array values.

Generics

Generics come in very handy when developing reusable components that can work against any data type. So, the client that consumes this component will decide what type of data it should act upon. Let's create a simple function that returns whatever data is passed to it:

```
function returnNumberReceived(arg: number): number {
    return arg;
}
function returnStringReceived(arg: string): string {
    return arg;
}
```

As you can see, we need individual methods to process each data type. We can implement the same in a single function using the `any` data type, as follows:

```
function returnAnythingReceived (arg: any): any {
    return arg;
}
```

This is similar to generics. However, we don't have control over the return type. If we pass a number and we can't predict whether the number will be returned or not by the function, The return type can be of any type.

Generics offer a special variable of the `T` type. Applying this type to the function, as shown, enables the client to pass the data type they would like this function to process:

```
function returnWhatReceived<T>(arg: T): T {
    return arg;
}
```

So, the client can call this function for various data types, as shown:

```
var stringOutput = returnWhatReceived<string>("return this"); // type of
output will be 'string'
var numberOutput = returnWhatReceived<number>(101); // type of output will
be number
```

Note that the data type to be processed is passed by wrapping it in angle brackets (<>) in the function call.

Generic interfaces

We can also define generic interfaces using the type variable `T`, as follows:

```
interface GenericFunc<T> {
    (arg: T): T;
}
function func<T>(arg: T): T {
    return arg;
}
var myFunc: GenericFunc<number> = func;
```

Here, we defined a generic interface and the `myFunc` variable of the `GenericFunc` type, passing the number data type for the type variable `T`. Then, this variable is assigned with a function named `func`.

Generic classes

Similar to generic interfaces, we can also define generic classes. We define classes with a generic type in angle brackets (<>), as shown:

```
class GenericClass<T> {
    add: (a: T, b: T) => T;
}
var myGenericClass = new GenericClass<number>();
myGenericClass.add = function(a, b) { return a + b; };
```

Here, the generic class is instantiated by passing the generic data type as number. So, the add function will process and add two numbers passed as parameters.

Decorators

Decorators enable us to extend a class or object by adding behaviors without modifying the code. Decorators wrap the class with extra functionality. They can be attached to a class, property, method, parameter, and accessor. In ECMAScript 2016, decorators are proposed to modify the behavior of a class. Decorators are prefixed with the @ symbol and a decorator name that resolves to a function called at runtime.

The following code snippet shows the authorize function, and it can be used as the @authorize decorator on any other class:

```
function authorize(target) {
    // check the authorization of the use to access the "target"
}
```

Class decorators

Class decorators are declared before the class declaration. Class decorators can observe, modify, and replace the definition of a class by applying to the constructor of that class. The signature of ClassDecorator in TypeScript is as illustrated:

```
declare type ClassDecorator = <TFunction extends Function>(target:
TFunction) => TFunction | void;
```

Consider a Customer class, and we would like that class to be freezed. Its existing properties should not be removed and new properties should not be added.

We can create a separate class that can take any object and freeze it. We can then decorate the customer class with @freezed to prevent adding new properties or removing the existing properties from the class:

```
@freezed
class Customer {
  public firstName: string;
  public lastName: string;
  constructor(firstName : string, lastName : string) {
    this.firstName = firstName;
    this.lastName = lastName;
  }
}
```

The preceding class takes four arguments in the firstname and lastname constructors. The following is the code snippet of the function written for the freezed decorator:

```
function freezed(target: any) {
    Object.freeze(target);
}
```

Here, the freezed decorator takes the target, that is, the Customer class that is being decorated and freezes it when it is executed.

Method decorators

Method decorators are declared before the method declaration. This decorator is used to modify, observe, or replace a method definition and is applied to the property descriptor for the method. The following code snippet shows a simple class with an applied method decorator:

```
class Hello {
    @logging
    increment(n: number) {
        return n++;
    }
}
```

The `Hello` class has the `increment` method that increments a number supplied to its parameter. Note that the `increment` method is decorated with the `@logging` decorator to log the input and output of the `increment` method. The following is the code snippet of the `logging` function:

```
function logging(target: Object, key: string, value: any) {
        value = function (...args: any[]) {
        var result = value.apply(this, args);
        console.log(JSON.stringify(args))
        return result;
    }
    };
}
```

The method decorator function takes three arguments: `target`, `key`, and `value`. The `target` argument holds the method that is being decorated; `key` holds the name of the method being decorated, and `value` is the property descriptor of the specified property if it exists on the object.

When the `increment` method is called, the `logging` decorator is invoked and the `values` parameters are passed to it. The `logging` method will log details about the arguments passed to the console.

Accessor decorators

Accessor decorators are prefixed before the accessor declaration. These decorators are used to observe, modify, or replace an accessor definition and are applied to the property descriptor. The following code snippet shows a simple class with the accessor decorator applied:

```
class Customer {
  private _firstname: string;
  private _lastname: string;
  constructor(firstname: string, lastname: string) {
        this._firstname = firstname;
        this._lastname = lastname;
  }
  @logging(false)
  get firstname() { return this._firstname; }
  @logging(false)
  get lastname() { return this._lastname; }
}
```

In this class, we decorate the get accessor of `firstname` and `lastname` with `@logging` and pass `boolean` to enable or disable logging. The following code snippet shows the function for the `@logging` decorator:

```
function logging(value: boolean) {
    return function (target: any, propertyKey: string, descriptor:
PropertyDescriptor) {
        descriptor.logging = value;
    };
}
```

The `logging` function sets the `Boolean` value to the `logging` property descriptor.

Property decorators

Property decorators are prefixed to property declarations. The signature of `PropertyDecorator` in the TypeScript source code is this:

```
declare type PropertyDecorator = (target: Object, propertyKey: string |
symbol) => void;
```

The following is a code snippet of a class with a property decorator applied to a property. In this code, the `firstname` property is decorated with the `@hashify` property decorator:

```
class Customer {
  @hashify
  public firstname: string;
  public lastname: string;
  constructor(firstname : string, lastname : string) {
    this.firstname = firstname;
    this.lastname = lastname;
  }
}
```

Now, we will see the code snippet of the @hashify property decorator function:

```
function hashify(target: any, key: string)
 {
  var _value = this[key];
  var getter = function ()
    {
        return '#' + _value;
    };
  var setter = function (newValue)
    {
        _value = newValue;
    };
  if (delete this[key])
  {
    Object.defineProperty(target, key,
  {
      get: getter,
      set: setter,
      enumerable: true,
      configurable: true
    });
  }
}
```

The _value variable holds the value of the property that is being decorated. Both the getter and setter functions will have access to the _value variable, and here, we can manipulate the _value variable by adding extra behaviors. I have concatenated # in getter to return hash tagged first name. Then, we delete the original property from the class prototype using the delete operator. A new property will be created with the original property name and the extra behavior.

Parameter decorators

Parameter decorators are prefixed to parameter declarations, and they are applied to a function for a class constructor or method declaration. This is the signature of ParameterDecorator:

```
declare type ParameterDecorator = (target: Object, propertyKey: string |
symbol, parameterIndex: number) => void;
```

Now, let's define the `Customer` class and use a parameter decorator to decorate a parameter in order to make it required, and validate whether the value has been served:

```
class Customer {
    constructor() {    }
    getName(@logging name: string) {
        return name;
    }
}
```

Here, the name parameter has been decorated with `@logging`. The parameter decorator implicitly takes three inputs, namely `prototype` of the class that has this decorator, `name` of the method that has this decorator, and `index` of the parameter that is being decorated. The `logging` function implementation of the parameter decorator is as illustrated:

```
function logging(target: any, key : string, index : number) {
  console.log(target);
  console.log(key);
  console.log(index);
}
```

Here, `target` is the class that has the decorator, `key` is the function name, and `index` contains the parameter index. This code just logs `target`, `key`, and `index` to the console.

TypeScript and Angular

As you have seen in this chapter, TypeScript comes with strong type-checking capabilities and supports object-oriented programming. Due to such advantages, the Angular team has chosen TypeScript to build Angular. Angular was completely rewritten from the core using TypeScript, and its architecture and coding pattern was completely changed, as you saw in `Chapter 2`, *Angular building blocks part 1*, and `Chapter 3`, *Angular building blocks part 2*. So, writing an Angular app using TypeScript is the best choice.

We can implement modules in Angular similar to modules in TypeScript. Components in an Angular application are actually a TypeScript class decorated with `@Component`. Modules can be imported to the current class file using import statements. The `export` keyword is used to indicate that this component can be imported and accessed in another module. The sample component code that is developed using TypeScript is as follows:

```
import {Component} from '@angular/core'
@Component({
  selector: 'my-component',
  template: '<h1>Hello my Component</h1>'
```

```
})
export class MyComponent {
  constructor() {  }
}
```

Summary

Voila! Now you've learned the fundamentals of the TypeScript language. We started by discussing what is TypeScript and its advantages. Then, you learned about the various data types in TypeScript with examples. We also walked through object-oriented programming in TypeScript and interfaces, classes, modules, functions, and generics with examples. Next, you learned about the various types of decorators and their implementation with examples. Finally, we saw why we should use TypeScript for Angular and the benefit of using TypeScript to write Angular applications.

In the next chapter, we will discuss how to create an Angular single-page application using Visual Studio.

5
Creating an Angular Single-Page Application in Visual Studio

This chapter guides you through the process of creating an Angular **Single Page Application (SPA)** using Visual Studio.

In this chapter, we will cover the following topics:

- Creating an ASP.NET Core web application
- Adding client-side packages using NPM package manager
- Using Gulp to run tasks
- Adding Angular components and templates

Creating an ASP.NET core web application

Let's start this chapter by creating an ASP.NET Core web application. I am assuming that you have Visual Studio 2017 or a later version installed in your development environment. Follow these steps to create the application:

1. Open Visual Studio and click on the menu item by navigating to `File | New | Project`.
2. Navigate to **Visual C#** from the installed template and select **Web**.

3. Then, select **ASP.NET Core Web Application** and enter the application name as My Todo, as shown in the following screenshot:

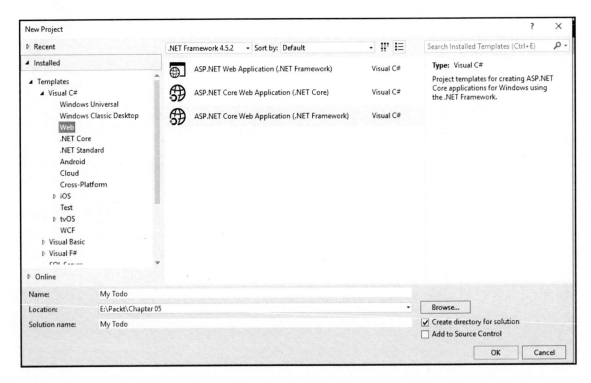

Creating a project named My Todo

4. Select the **ASP.NET Core Empty** template and click on **Ok** to create the project, as illustrated:

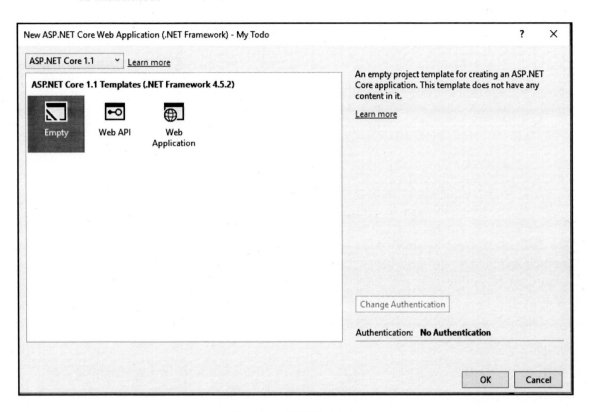

Select an empty ASP.NET Core template

The solution structure of the `My Todo` application that we created is shown in the following screenshot:

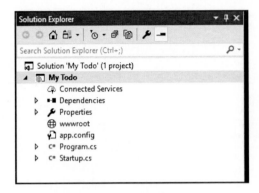

The default solution structure of My Todo

The `Startup` class is the entry point of an ASP.NET Core web application. The `Configure` method in the `Startup` class is used to set up a request pipeline to handle all the requests coming to the application. Here, the default code of the `Startup` class is configured to return the `Hello World!` text by default:

```csharp
1 reference
public class Startup
{
    // This method gets called by the runtime. Use this method to add services to the container.
    // For more information on how to configure your application, visit https://go.microsoft.com/fwlink/?LinkID=398940
    0 references
    public void ConfigureServices(IServiceCollection services)
    {
    }

    // This method gets called by the runtime. Use this method to configure the HTTP request pipeline.
    0 references
    public void Configure(IApplicationBuilder app, IHostingEnvironment env, ILoggerFactory loggerFactory)
    {
        loggerFactory.AddConsole();

        if (env.IsDevelopment())
        {
            app.UseDeveloperExceptionPage();
        }

        app.Run(async (context) =>
        {
            await context.Response.WriteAsync("Hello World!");
        });
    }
}
```

The default code of the Startup class

So, when you run the application, you will get the following output in the browser:

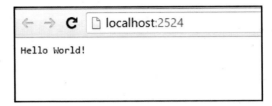

The default output of the 'My Todo' project

Now, let's make the application to serve a default page for any request coming through. Follow these steps to do so:

1. Select the `wwwroot` folder under the `My Todo` project. Right-click on selecting the project and navigate to **Add** and click **New Item**:

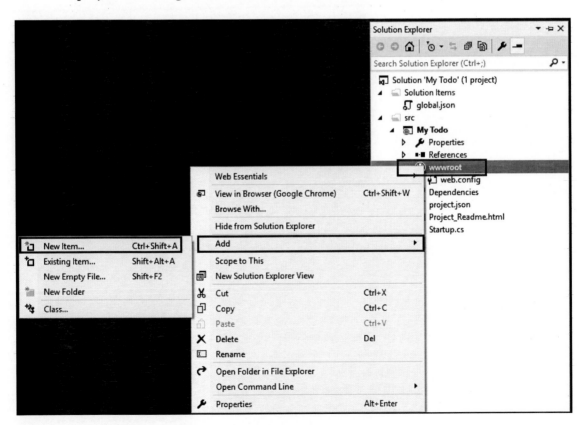

Navigate to the Add New Item menu

2. In the **Add New Item** window, click on **Content** under **Web**, and then select **HTML Page** from the center pane. Enter `index.html` as the filename and click on **Add**:

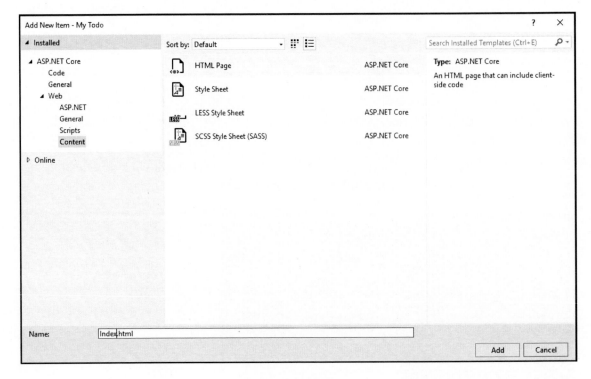

Name the HTML file as index.html

3. Update the content of the index.html file, as follows:

```
index.html  ⊐  ✕
            <!DOCTYPE html>
        ⊟<html>
        ⊟<head>
                <meta charset="utf-8" />
                <title>My Todo</title>
            </head>
        ⊟<body>
                <h1>My Todo Landing Page</h1>
            </body>
            </html>
```

The updated code of index.html

4. Open the Startup class and delete the following code snippet that writes the Hello World default text to a response for each request:

```
app.Run(async (context) =>
{
       await    context.Response.WriteAsync("Hello
       World!");
});
```

5. Add the following code to the Configure method so that the pipeline serves default and static files to the request:

```
public void Configure(IApplicationBuilder app)
{
       app.UseIISPlatformHandler();

       app.UseDefaultFiles();
       app.UseStaticFiles();
}
```

The code to enable the pipeline to serve static and default files

6. You need to add the `Microsoft.AspNetCore.StaticFiles` NuGet package, as shown, in order to use these extensions:

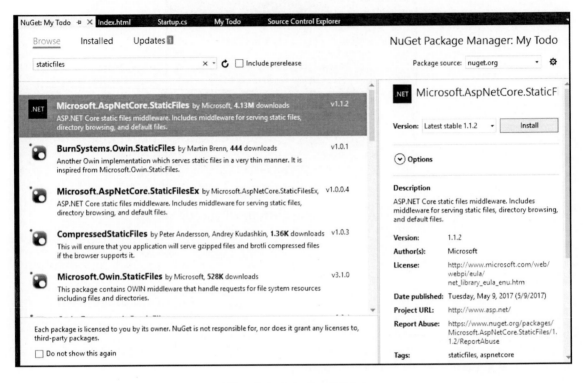

Adding a reference to a namespace if required

7. Now, add an `index.html` file under the `wwwroot` folder and run the application by pressing *F5*. You will note that the application serves the `index.html` file as the default file for the request. Here, I have added an `h1` tag with the content **My Todo Landing Page**:

The output of the application after adding index.html

Adding client-side packages using NPM package manager

When we develop applications, we add references to many frameworks and libraries as dependencies. In Visual Studio, we have the NuGet package manager tool to manage all those packages in our application.

In the frontend web community, using Bower, Grunt, Gulp, and NPM to manage packages and running build tasks to develop modern web applications has become widely popular. As this ecosystem is very rich and widely accepted, Visual Studio 2015 has adopted these systems to manage client-side frameworks and libraries, as illustrated. NuGet is ideal to manage server-side packages:

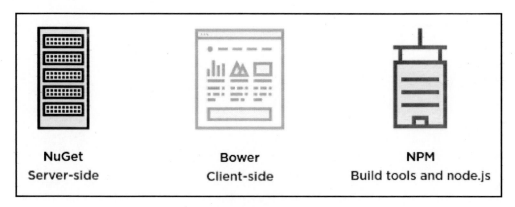

| NuGet | Bower | NPM |
| Server-side | Client-side | Build tools and node.js |

Various package managing tools

We saw how to manage client-side packages using NPM in Visual Studio Code. Similarly, we use NPM in Visual Studio 2015 or later to manage frontend frameworks and libraries in our project. Let's add the Angular framework and other required JavaScript libraries as dependencies to our project using NPM by following these steps:

1. First, let's add **NPM Configuration File** to our project. Right-click on the project node and navigate to Add | New Item. Select **General** under **Web** from the left-hand side pane and **NPM Configuration File** from the middle pane.

Then, click on **Add**, leaving the default name as `package.json`:

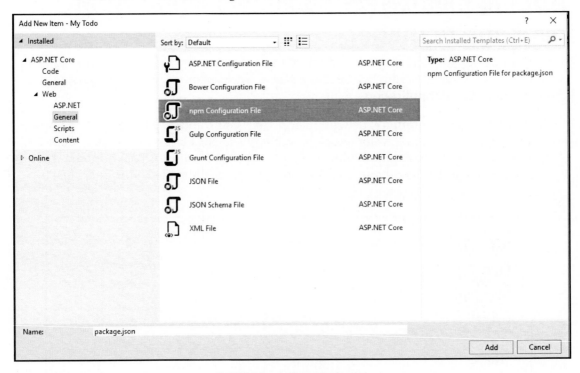

The NPM configuration file named package.json

The `package.json` file will be added to your project with the following default JSON code:

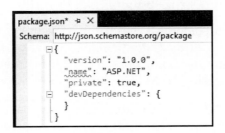

The code snippet of package.json

2. Update the `name` field with `my-todo` and add the required dependencies to the `package.json` file, as shown:

```
"version": "1.0.0",
"name": "my-todo",
"private": true,
```

```
"dependencies":
{
  "@angular/common": "~4.0.0",
  "@angular/compiler": "~4.0.0",
  "@angular/core": "~4.0.0",
  "@angular/forms": "~4.0.0",
  "@angular/platform-browser": "~4.0.0",
  "@angular/platform-browser-dynamic":    "~4.0.0",
  "systemjs": "0.19.40",
  "core-js": "^2.4.1",
  "rxjs": "5.0.1",
  "zone.js": "^0.8.4"
},
  "devDependencies":
{
  "@types/node": "^6.0.46",
  "typescript": "~2.1.0"
}
}
```

3. The moment we save package.json with all the dependency information, Visual Studio adds the required packages to our project under the node_modules hidden folder, and you can see the list of loaded dependencies by navigating to the npm folder under the Dependencies node, as illustrated in the following screenshot:

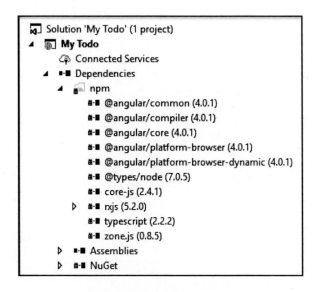

The NPM folder with dependency libraries

We have all the client-side frameworks and libraries in our project dependency node that we need. However, we need to add the dependent libraries to our `wwwroot` folder for our application to refer and consume. We will discuss this in the next section.

Using Gulp to run tasks

Gulp is a task runner that runs on `node.js`. Using Gulp, we can automate activities such as moving or copying files, and bundling and minification. In ASP.NET Core, Microsoft also integrated Gulp with Visual Studio as it has been widely accepted by the web community to run and manage complex tasks very easily. You can find more information by visiting the official site at `http://gulpjs.com/`

Let's use Gulp to push the required JavaScript frameworks and libraries from the `node_modules` folder hidden in the solution to the `libs` folder under `wwwroot`. Installing Gulp in Visual Studio is easy. Perform the following steps to install and run Gulp tasks:

1. Add Gulp as a dev dependency in the `package.json` NPM configuration file, as shown, and save the file:

```
{
    "version": "1.0.0",
    "name": "my-todo",
    "private": true,
    "dependencies": {
    "@angular/common": "~4.0.0",
    "@angular/compiler": "~4.0.0",
    "@angular/core": "~4.0.0",
    "@angular/forms": "~4.0.0",
    "@angular/platform-browser": "~4.0.0",
    "@angular/platform-browser-dynamic":
    "~4.0.0",
    "systemjs": "0.19.40",
    "core-js": "^2.4.1",
    "rxjs": "5.0.1",
    "zone.js": "^0.8.4"
},
    "devDependencies": {
    "@types/node": "^6.0.46",
    "gulp": "^3.9.1",
    "typescript": "~2.1.0"
    }
}
```

When we save the `package.json` file with Gulp added in the dev dependencies, Visual Studio installs the package into our application under the node `Dependencies | npm` folder, as in the following screenshot:

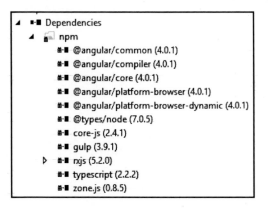

The Gulp dependency under the added npm folder

We have the gulp package in our application. Now, we need to write a task in JavaScript to copy the required JavaScript libraries from the `node_modules` folder that is hidden in a solution, as follows:

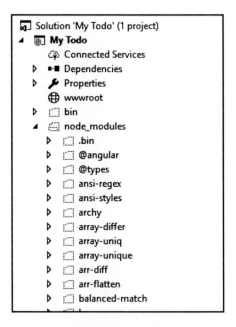

The node_modules hidden folder

2. Now, let's add the **Gulp Configuration File** to our project. Right-click on the project and navigate to Add | New Item. Select **General** under **Web** on the left-hand side pane, and then select **Gulp Configuration File** from the middle pane. Then, click on **Add**, leaving the default name as gulpfile.js:

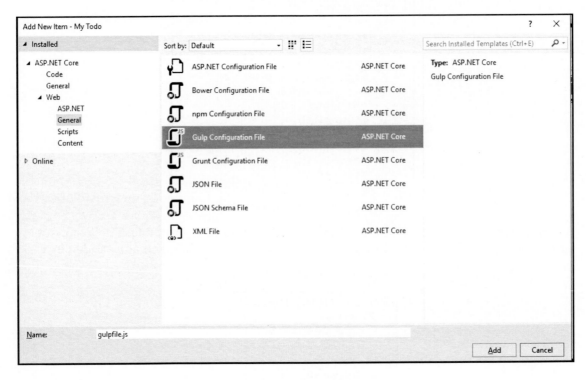

Adding the Gulp configuration file

The default content of the Gulp configuration file `gulpfile.js` is as follows:

```
/*
This file in the main entry point for defining Gulp tasks and using Gulp plugins.
Click here to learn more. http://go.microsoft.com/fwlink/?LinkId=518007
*/

var gulp = require('gulp');

gulp.task('default', function () {
    // place code for your default task here
});
```

The default code snippet of the Gulp configuration file

3. Let's write another task to copy the required JavaScript libraries from the `node_modules` hidden folder to the `libs` folder under the `wwwroot` node of the project. Add the following code snippet to `gulpfile.js` for the new task:

```
var paths = {
    sourcePath: "./node_modules",
    targetPath: "./wwwroot/libs"
}
    var librariesToMove = [
    paths.sourcePath + '/core-
js/client/shim.min.js',
    paths.sourcePath + '/zone.js/dist/zone.min.js',
    paths.sourcePath +
    '/systemjs/dist/system.src.js',
];
    var gulp = require('gulp');
    gulp.task('librariesToMove',    function () {
    return
    gulp.src(librariesToMove).pipe
    (gulp.dest(paths.targetPath));
});
```

The `paths` variable holds the source and target folder of the libraries to be moved, and the `librariesToMove` variable holds the list of libraries to be moved to the `libs` folder. The last statement in the file is the new task that copies the required JavaScript libraries to the `libs` folder when it is run.

4. We have the code for the Gulp task ready, and now, we need to run the Gulp task to copy the libraries. So, to run the task, open **Task Runner Explorer** by right-clicking on `gulpfile.js`, as shown in the following screenshot:

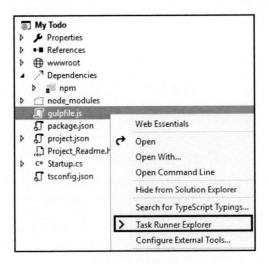

Opening Task Runner Explorer

Task Runner Explorer will list the available tasks written in `gulpfile.js` as a child tree node under **Tasks**, as in the screenshot here:

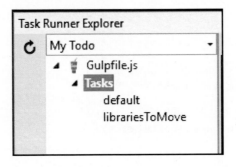

The list of tasks available in gulpfile.js

5. Right-click on the `librariesToMove` task listed in **Task Runner Explorer** and select **Run** from the menu, as follows:

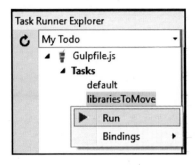

Running the librariesToMove task in gulpfile.js

You can see the command getting executed to run the task on the right-hand side pane of **Task Runner Explorer**:

```
> cmd.exe /c gulp -b "D:\Packt\My Todo\src\My Todo" --color --gulpfile "D:\Packt\My Todo\src\My Todo
\Gulpfile.js" librariesToMove
[10:11:00] Using gulpfile
[10:11:00] Starting 'librariesToMove'...
Process terminated with code 0.
[10:11:05] Finished 'librariesToMove' after
```

The task completed with zero errors

Note that the libraries are copied to `wwwroot` under the `libs` folder, as illustrated in the following screenshot:

The libs folder created with the required JavaScript libraries

6. Now that we have the required libraries under the `libs` folder in the `wwwroot` node, let's update `index.html` by adding both the script references to the libraries in the `libs` folder and the code to configure `SystemJS`, as demonstrated:

```
<!DOCTYPE html>
<html>
<head>
    <title>My   Todo</title>
    <script>document.write('<base    href="' +
    document.location +
    '" />');</script>
    <meta charset="UTF-8">
    <!-- Polyfills -->
    <script src="libs/shim.min.js"></script>
    <script src="libs/zone.min.js"></script>
    <script src="libs/system.src.js"></script>
    <script src="systemjs.config.js"></script>
    <script>
      System.import('main.js').catch(function(err){
      console.error(err); });
    </script>
</head>
<body>
    <my-app>Loading My Todo   App...</my-app>
</body>
</html>
```

7. Add a `system.js` configuration file `systemjs.config.js` and update it with the following content. This has the mapping information to load the angular libraries when running the applications:

```
(function (global) {
System.config({
paths: {
'npm:': 'node_modules/'
},
map: {
'app': 'app',
'@angular/common':
'npm:@angular/common/bundles/common.umd.js',
'@angular/compiler':
'npm:@angular/compiler/bundles/compiler.umd.js',
'@angular/core':
'npm:@angular/core/bundles/core.umd.js',
'@angular/forms':
'npm:@angular/forms/bundles/forms.umd.js',
```

```
'@angular/platform-browser': 'npm:@angular/platform-
browser/bundles/platform-browser.umd.js',
'@angular/platform-browser-dynamic':
'npm:@angular/platform-
browser-dynamic/bundles/platform-browser-
dynamic.umd.js',
'rxjs': 'npm:rxjs'
},
packages:
{app: {
main: './main.js',
defaultExtension: 'js'
},
rxjs: {
defaultExtension: 'js'
}
}
});
})(this);
```

We created a project to develop the My Todo application and managed all the client-side dependencies using NPM package manager. We also used Gulp to run a task in order to copy JavaScript libraries to the wwwroot node. In the next section, let's create the required Angular components for our application.

Adding Angular components and templates

We will be writing Angular components for our application using TypeScript. The TypeScript files should be compiled to JavaScript, targeting ECMAScript 5.

Configuring TypeScript compiler options

We need to inform Visual Studio about the compiler options required to compile TypeScript for our application to consume when it is running. With the help of a TypeScript configuration file, we can configure the compiler options and other details using the following steps:

1. Let's add **TypeScript Configuration File** by right-clicking on the project and navigating to Add | New Item in the menu, leaving the filename to default, as shown in this screenshot:

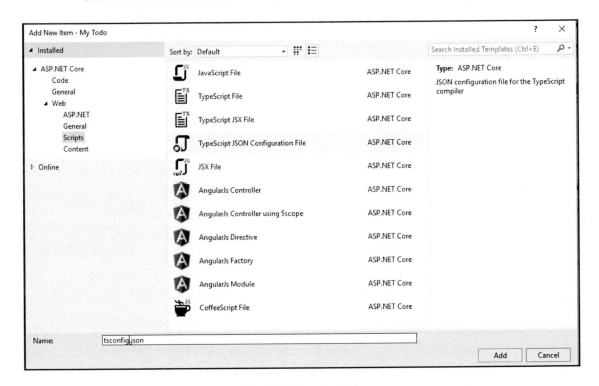

Adding the TypeScript configuration file

A file named tsconfig.json will be added to the project root directory.

2. Replace the content of the TypeScript configuration file with the following configuration:

```
{
    "compilerOptions":
    {
```

```
"diagnostics": true,
"emitDecoratorMetadata":    true,
"experimentalDecorators":    true,
"lib": ["es2015", "dom"],
"listFiles": true,
"module": "commonjs",
"moduleResolution": "node",
"noImplicitAny": true,
"outDir": "wwwroot",
"removeComments": false,
"rootDir": "wwwroot",
"sourceMap": true,
"suppressImplicitAnyIndexErrors":    true,
"target": "es5"
},
"exclude": [
"node_modules"
]
}
```

Adding an Angular component

We configured the project with TypeScript compiler options. Now, let's add an Angular root component for our application. Follow these steps to do so:

1. First, create an app folder under wwwroot by right-clicking on it and navigate to Add | New Folder, as shown in the following screenshot:

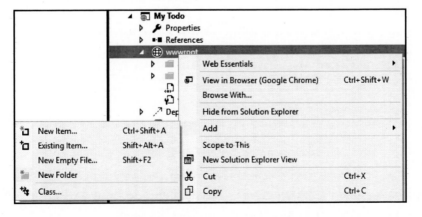

Adding a new folder named app for the Angular application folder

2. We have the `app` folder ready. Let's add the TypeScript file to create a root component by right-clicking on the `app` folder and navigating to Add | New Item. Select **Scripts** under **Web** from the left-hand side pane and select **TypeScript File** from the middle pane. Name the file as the `app.component.ts` file and click on **Add**:

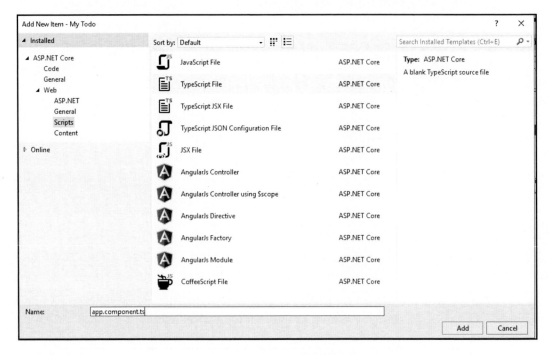

Adding a root component named app.component.ts

3. Add the following code snippet to `app.component.ts`:

```
import { Component } from '@angular/core';
@Component({
    selector: 'my-app',
    template: `<h1>Hello    {{name}}</h1>`
})
export class AppComponent { name   = 'My Todo App';
}
```

A root component named `AppComponent` is created and decorated with the component metadata `selector` and `templateUrl`.

Adding app module

In the preceding section, we created an Angular component named `AppComponent`. Now we need to bootstrap this `AppComponent` so that Angular will consider this as a root component of the application. We can bootstrap a component by decorating an `AppModule` class with the `NgModule` and adding the metadata bootstrap assigned with `AppComponent`. Follow these steps to create `AppModule`:

1. Create a `TypeScript` by right-clicking on the app folder and navigating to Add | New Item. Select **Scripts** under **Web** from the left-hand side pane and select **TypeScript File** from the middle pane. Add a file named `app.module.ts`, and click on **Add**:

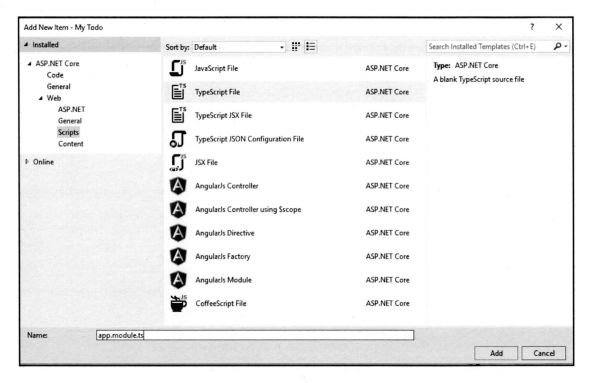

Adding the TypeScript file named app.module.ts

2. Add the following code snippet to `app.module.ts`:

```
import { NgModule } from '@angular/core';
import { BrowserModule } from '@angular/platform-
browser';
import { FormsModule } from '@angular/forms';
import { AppComponent } from './app.component';
@NgModule({
imports: [
BrowserModule,
FormsModule
],
declarations: [AppComponent],
bootstrap: [AppComponent]
})
export class AppModule { }
```

Here, we added `AppComponent` as root component and imported `BrowserModule` as our application will be consumed via browser and `FormsModule` two bindings.

Adding an Angular component

Now we need to bootstrap the `AppModule` created in the preceding section. Perform the following steps:

1. Let's create a `TypeScript` file, `main.ts`, to bootstrap `AppModule`. Right-click on the `wwwroot` folder and navigate to `Add | New Item`. Select **Scripts** under **Web** on the left-hand side pane and select **TypeScript File** from the middle pane. Name the file as `main.ts`, and click on **Add**:

Adding the TypeScript file named main.ts

2. Update the `main.ts` file with this code snippet:

```
import { platformBrowserDynamic }    from
'@angular/platform-
browser-dynamic';
import { AppModule } from './app/app.module';
platformBrowserDynamic().bootstrapModule(AppModule);
```

Here, platform browser dynamic contains angular features that make the app run in the browser by bootstrapping application module. We can ignore this if our application is not targeting to run on the browser.

We have all that we need to verify that our Angular application is running properly. Note how nicely Visual Studio has organized the template files, TypeScript files, and their respective compiled JavaScript files under the solution explorer, as shown in the following screenshot:

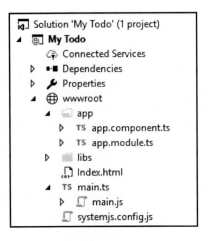

Compiled TypeScript files to JavaScript files

Note that Visual Studio will automatically generate JavaScript files after compiling the TypeScript files in the app folder as and when you make changes and save the files.

3. Let's run the application by pressing *F5*, and, if it builds successfully, you will get to see the output in the browser, as shown in the following screenshot:

The output of the application

Note that the inner text of the `<my-app>` tag is inserted with the content in `app.component.html`.

Adding a Todo class

Our application deals with Todo items. So, let's create a class named Todo and add properties such as title and completed to it, as illustrated:

```
export class Todo {
    title: string;
    completed: boolean;
    constructor(title: string) {
        this.title = title;
        this.completed = false;
    }
    set isCompleted(value:   boolean) {
        this.completed = value;
    }
}
```

This Todo class also has a constructor that takes title as a parameter and a method that sets the todo item as completed.

Adding a TodoService class

Now, let's create a TodoService class that acts as a service repository to manage todo items. The following is the code snippet of the todo.service.ts file:

```
import { Todo } from './todo'
export class TodoService {
    todos: Array<Todo>
    constructor() {
        this.todos = [new Todo('First   item'),
        new Todo('Second item'),
        new Todo('Third item')];
    }
    getPending() {
        return   this.todos.filter((todo: Todo) => todo.completed ===
        false);
    }
    getCompleted() {
        return   this.todos.filter((todo: Todo) => todo.completed ===
        true);
    }
    remove(todo: Todo) {
            this.todos.splice(this.todos.indexOf(todo), 1);
    }
    add(title: string) {
```

```
            this.todos.push(new    Todo(title));
    }
    toggleCompletion(todo: Todo)     {
        todo.completed =    !todo.completed;
    }
    removeCompleted() {
        this.todos =    this.getPending();
    }
}
```

We have created the `TodoService` class with various methods to add, remove, and return
the collection of `todo` items.

Updating the AppComponent class

Now that we have the `TodoService` class in place, let's update the `AppComponent` class, as
shown, to consume the `TodoService` class:

```
import { Component } from '@angular/core';
import { Todo } from './todo'
import { TodoService } from './todo.service'
@Component({
    selector: 'my-app',
    templateUrl: './app/app.component.html'
})
export class AppComponent {
    todos: Array<Todo>;
    todoService: TodoService;
    newTodoText = '';
    constructor(todoService:    TodoService) {
        this.todoService =    todoService;
        this.todos =    todoService.todos;
    }
    removeCompleted() {
        this.todoService.removeCompleted();
    }
    toggleCompletion(todo: Todo)     {
        this.todoService.toggleCompletion(todo);
    }
    remove(todo: Todo) {
        this.todoService.remove(todo);
    }
    addTodo() {
        if   (this.newTodoText.trim().length) {
            this.todoService.add(this.newTodoText);
          this.newTodoText = '';
```

```
                }
            }
        }
```

Note that the metadata `template` in the `@Component` has been replaced with the `templateUrl` and is assigned with an `AppComponent` template file `app.component.html`. As the template content is complex now, we need to introduce an HTML file for the `AppComponent` view.

Updating the AppModule

We need to tell the injector that it needs to inject `TodoService` when `AppComponent` is constructed. So, to let the injector know about the `TodoService` class, we need to add `TodoService` as provider in `AppModule` to supply `TodoService` when it is required by the `AppComponent`. The following code snippet shows the updated `app.module.ts` file:

```
import { NgModule } from '@angular/core';
import { BrowserModule } from '@angular/platform-browser';
import { FormsModule } from '@angular/forms';
import { AppComponent } from './app.component';
import { TodoService } from './todo.service'
@NgModule({
    imports: [
        BrowserModule,
        FormsModule
    ],
    declarations: [AppComponent],
    providers: [TodoService],
    bootstrap: [AppComponent]
})
export class AppModule { }
```

Adding the AppComponent template

We have the required properties and methods in the AppComponent class. Now, let's add the template to show a todo list, a textbox to get the title of a todo item from the user, an add button to add a new todo item, a checkbox for each todo item to mark them as completed, a button for each todo item to delete them, and a button at the bottom of the template to remove the completed todo items from the todo list. The following is the updated code snippet of AppComponent with all the mentioned features:

```
<section>
    <header>
        <h1>todos</h1>
        <input placeholder="Add   new todo" autofocus=""
[(ngModel)]="newTodoText">
        <button type="button"    (click)="addTodo()">Add</button>
    </header>
    <section *ngIf="todoService.todos.length    > 0">
        <ul>
            <li *ngFor="let   todo of todoService.todos">
                <input type="checkbox"    (click)="toggleCompletion(todo)"
[checked]="todo.completed">
                    <label>{{todo.title}}</label>
                <button    (click)="remove(todo)">X</button>
            </li>
        </ul>
    </section>
    <footer *ngIf="todoService.todos.length    > 0">
        <span><strong>{{todoService.getPending().length}}</strong>
{{todoService.getPending().length == 1 ? 'item' : 'items'}} left</span>
        <button *ngIf="todoService.getCompleted().length    > 0"
(click)="removeCompleted()">Clear completed</button>
    </footer>
</section>
```

As you can see, we applied two-way binding using ngModel to the input control in order to bind the new todo item, title. We assigned the addTodo method to the click event of the Add button to add a new todo item to the in-memory collection of Todo items in todoService. We applied ngFor to the <li> tag to iterate each Todo item in todoService. The checkbox rendered for each Todo item has its click event, the checked property mapped with the toggleCompletion method, and a completed property of the Todo item, respectively. Next, the remove button has its click event mapped with the remove method in AppComponent.

The footer tag has a span that displays the pending `Todo` items' count and a button to remove the completed `todo` items from the list. This button has a `click` event mapped with the `removeCompleted` method in `AppComponent`.

Let's run the application by pressing *F5*, and you will be able to perform all the operations, such as adding, removing, and listing `todo` items:

My Todo App operations

Summary

Hurray! You actually learned the very important and core objective of the book in this chapter. Yes! I am talking about integrating Angular with .NET applications.

We started the chapter by creating a new ASP.NET Core empty application and updated the `Startup` class to serve static and default pages for any request. Then, you learned about managing client-side packages using NPM in Visual Studio, and we managed to automate and run tasks using Gulp in Visual Studio. Next, you learned how to add the required components for the application and bootstrap it. Later, we designed a model class and a service class that handle the core business logic of the application. Finally, we designed a template to list the `Todo` items, and also, we added a few controls and hooked them to certain methods in `TodoService` and `AppComponent`.

This application only deals with the in-memory todo items. However, in the real-time application, we consume a service to add, delete, or fetch the `todo` items. In the next chapter, we will discuss how to create an ASP.NET Core Web API service that handles retrieving, saving, and deleting `todo` items and also consuming it from our Angular application that we just built.

6

Creating ASP.NET Core Web API Services for Angular

This chapter takes you through the process of creating ASP.NET Web API services for Angular applications that we created in the last chapter.

In this chapter, we will cover the following topics:

- RESTful Web Services
- ASP.NET Web API overview
- Creating ASP.NET Web API services
- Integrating the ASP.NET Web API with Angular applications

RESTful Web Services

Representational State Transfer (REST) is an architectural style or design principle that can be applied to implement RESTful services. REST ensures that the communication between clients and services is improved by having a limited number of operations. REST helps you organize these communications between independent systems in a simple way.

In REST, each resource is identified by its own **Universal Resource Identifier (URI)**. It uses HTTP under the hood and utilizes HTTP verbs, such as GET, POST, PUT, and DELETE, to control or access the resources.

RESTful web services are stateless in nature and are easy to scale. They work under the HTTP protocol and can be accessed from any device that supports HTTP. A client need not worry about anything other than the data format:

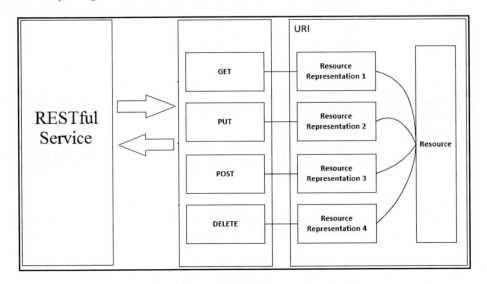

A RESTful service

ASP.NET Web API Overview

The ASP.NET Web API is a framework that can be used to build RESTful services on the .NET framework. The ASP.NET Web API is based on the HTTP protocol, and it exposes the HTTP verbs/actions in the form of a URI, allowing client applications to interact with data using HTTP verbs. Any client application or device that supports HTTP communications can easily access Web API services.

As discussed in the preceding section, the RESTful service will identify resources through a URI. For example, we have `http://www.programmerguide.net/api/todos/101`, and an Angular application applies a GET request. The C# method that responds to this GET request will be on a web API controller class. The routing technique will take care of mapping the request URI with the respective controller and methods based on the route configured or annotated in the respective classes and methods.

Here, the request will be handled by a `Get` method in `TodosController` according to the default configurations. The `Get` method will retrieve the `Todo` item based on the ID value 101 from the database and return it as a `Todo` object. The returned `Todo` object will be serialized to JSON or XML.

In case of the `Post` method, a newly posted `Todo` object will be received from the request body in the form of JSON and will be deserialized into the `Todo` object in order to use it inside the `Post` method of `TodosController`.

We can create HTTP-based services through the powerful ASP.NET **Model-View-Controller** (**MVC**) programming model in the ASP.NET Web API. Features such as routing, model binding, and validation provide greater flexibility in developing RESTful web services using the ASP.NET Web API.

Why the ASP.NET Web API is a great fit for Angular

The ASP.NET Web API is a framework that can be used to build HTTP services. It is built with very lightweight architecture, and it can be accessed asynchronously using an HTTP service in Angular in a RESTful way. Using the ASP.NET Web API, we can easily synchronize data in Angular applications.

Creating ASP.NET Web API services

Let's create or add ASP.NET Web API services to our My Todo application that we created in the last chapter. Our My Todo application was created using the Empty ASP.NET 5 template in Visual Studio 2015. When an empty project is created, it creates a lean web application. It does not include assemblies related to MVC or the Web API. So, we need to explicitly add the required assemblies or modules to implement the Web API in our application.

Adding and configuring an MVC service to the ASP.NET project

Since ASP.NET Core, the Web API, was merged with MVC, we need to add an MVC service to implement a Web API in our application:

1. Install the NuGet package Microsoft.AspNetCore.MVC.
2. Open the Startup.cs file from the root folder of the project in Visual Studio.
3. Add the following statement under the ConfigureServices method to add the MVC service to our project

```
public void    ConfigureServices(IServiceCollection
services)
    {
        services.AddMvc();
    }
```

4. We just enabled MVC in our project. Next, we will wire up MVC with our request pipeline by adding the following statement in the Configure method:

```
app.UseMvc();
```

Adding Web API Controller to an ASP.NET application

We just enabled and wired up the MVC service to our application. Now, let's add a Web API controller by following these steps:

1. Right-click on the My Todo project, navigate to Add | New Folder, and name the folder Controllers:

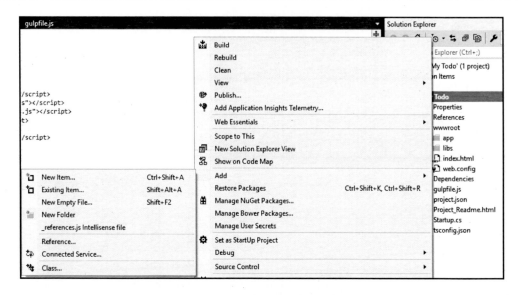

Create a new folder for controllers under the My Todo project

2. Now, right-click on the `Controllers` folder that we just created and go to Add |
New Item:

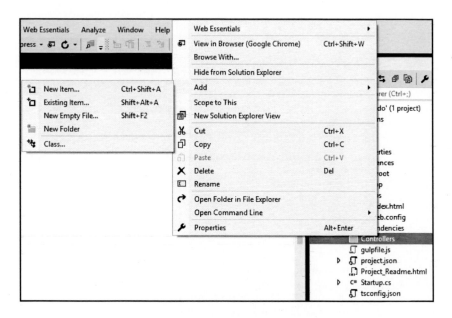

Add the Web API controller to the Controllers folder

3. Select **Minimal Dependencies** and click on **Add** if you get an Add MVC Dependencies popup:

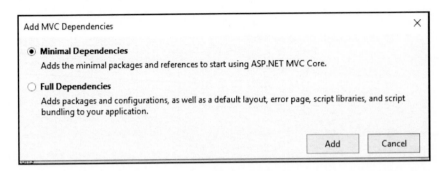

Add minimal MVC dependencies

Visual Studio 2017 has added a `ScaffoldingReadMe.txt` readme file with the following instructions to enable scaffolding in our application; follow and update your project code accordingly.

ASP.NET MVC core dependencies have been added to the project. However, you may still need to make these changes to your project:

1. Add `Scaffolding CLI` tool to the project:

```
<ItemGroup>
 <DotNetCliToolReference
 Include="Microsoft.VisualStudio.Web.CodeGeneration.
 Tools"  Version="1.0.0" />
</ItemGroup>
```

2. These are the suggested changes to the `Startup` class:

```
2.1 Add a constructor:
    public IConfigurationRoot   Configuration { get; }
    public Startup(IHostingEnvironment   env)
    {
        var builder = new   ConfigurationBuilder()
            .SetBasePath(env.ContentRootPath)
            .AddJsonFile("appsettings.json",
             optional: true,
                reloadOnChange: true)
            .AddJsonFile($"appsettings.
             {env.EnvironmentName}.json",   optional:
              true)
            .AddEnvironmentVariables();
```

```
        Configuration =    builder.Build();
   }
2.2 Add MVC services:
   public void    ConfigureServices(IServiceCollection
   services)
   {
       // Add framework    services.
       services.AddMvc();
  }
2.3 Configure web app to use    use Configuration and
   use MVC routing:
    public void    Configure(IApplicationBuilder app,
   IHostingEnvironment env, ILoggerFactory
   loggerFactory)
       {
   loggerFactory.AddConsole(Configuration.GetSection
   ("Logging"));
         loggerFactory.AddDebug();
       if (env.IsDevelopment())
       {
             app.UseDeveloperExceptionPage();
       }
       else
       {
             app.UseExceptionHandler("/Home/Error");
       }
       app.UseStaticFiles();
       app.UseMvc(routes    =>
       {
           routes.MapRoute(
               name: "default",
               template: "
   {controller=Home}/{action=Index}
               /{id?}");
       });
   }
```

3. Again, right-click on the `Controllers` folder, go to **Add | Controllers**, select **API Controller with read/write actions**, and name it as `TodosController`:

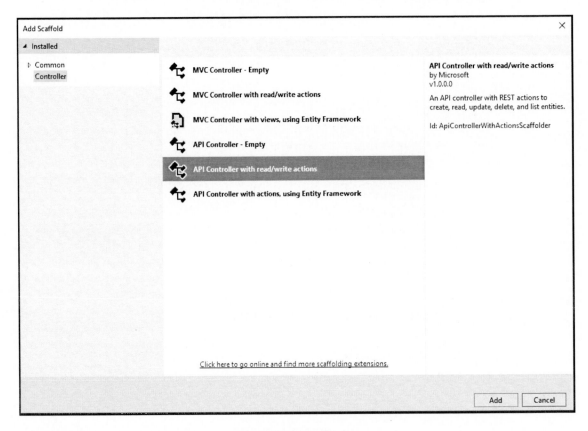

Name the controller TodosController

 If you get the error in the following screenshot, you need to add the given XML tag by editing your `csproj` file and then, add the controller again.

This is the error:

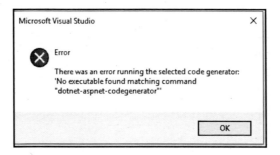

The following is the code for the XML tag:

```
<ItemGroup>
        <DotNetCliToolReference
Include="Microsoft.VisualStudio.Web.CodeGeneration.Tools"    Version="1.0.1"
/>
</ItemGroup>
```

This will create the `TodosController` Web API controller with the following template code for us to modify according to our needs:

```
[Produces("application/json")]
    [Route("api/Todos")]
    public class TodosController    : Controller
    {
        // GET: api/Todos
        [HttpGet]
        public    IEnumerable<string> Get()
        {
            return new string[] {    "value1", "value2" };
        }
        // GET: api/Todos/5
        [HttpGet("{id}", Name = "Get")]
        public string Get(int id)
        {
            return "value";
        }
        // POST: api/Todos
        [HttpPost]
        public void    Post([FromBody]string value)
        {
        }
        // PUT: api/Todos/5
        [HttpPut("{id}")]
        public void Put(int id,    [FromBody]string value)
```

```
        {
        }
        // DELETE:    api/ApiWithActions/5
        [HttpDelete("{id}")]
        public void Delete(int    id)
        {
        }
    }
```

4. Press *F5* to run the application and navigate to
    `http://localhost:2524/api/todos` from the browser.

You may have a different port in your system.

You will see the following output from `TodosController` as per the default
code in the `Get` method. As you can see in the following screenshot, it just
returned an array of string:

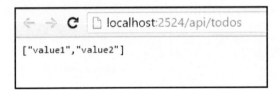

The output of the default Get action in TodoController

Adding models to an ASP.NET application

We configured our application to use MVC services and added the Web API controller. Now, let's add the models needed for our My Todo application. Follow these steps to add a model named `Todo`:

1. Right-click on the `My Todo` project, navigate to **Add** | **New Folder**, and name the folder `Models`:

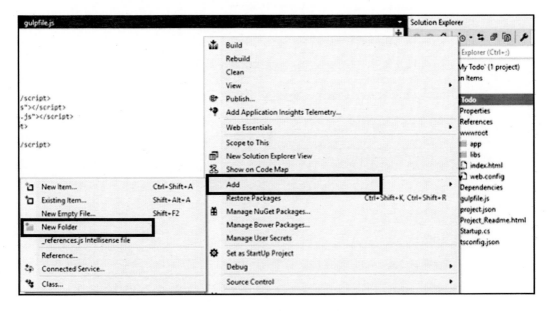

Add a new folder for Models under the My Todo project

2. Now, right-click on the `Models` folder that we just created and go to **Add** | **Class**....:

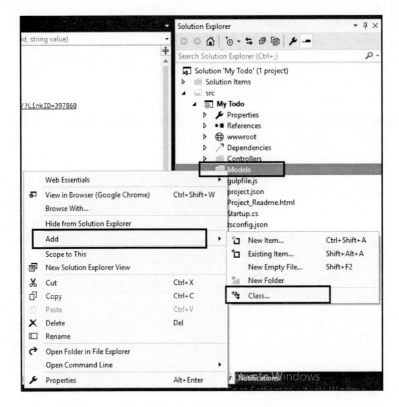

Add a class for the Todo object under the Models folder

3. Name the class `Todo` and add the following code snippet to it:

```
namespace My_Todo.Models
{
public class Todo
{
public int Id { get; set;
  }
public string Title { get; set;
  }
public bool Completed { get; set;
  }
 }
}
```

`Todo` is a C# POCO class that represents a `Todo` item. It has properties such as an `Id` that holds the primary key value of the `Todo` item, the `Title` property that holds the title of the `Todo` item, and the `Completed` property that holds the Boolean flag to indicate whether the item is completed.

Adding DBContext to an ASP.NET application

We just added the `Todo` model. Now, let's add `DBContext` to manage and persist `Todo` in the database. `DBContext` acts as a bridge between your classes and database. To add it, follow these steps:

1. Right-click on the `Models` folder and navigate to **Add** | **Class**:

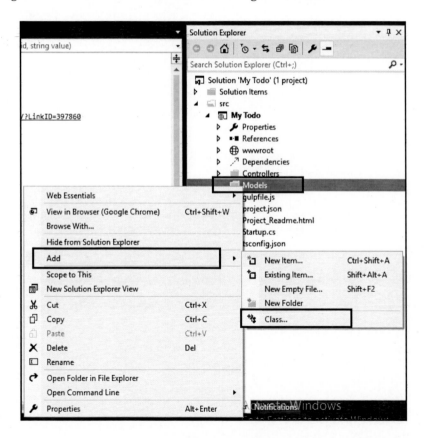

Add a class for DBContext under the Models folder

2. Name the class as `TodoContext` and add the following code snippet to it:

```
public class TodoContext : DbContext
{
  public TodoContext (DbContextOptions<TodoContext>
  options)
  : base(options)
  {
  }
  public DbSet<Todo> Todos { get; set; }
}
```

`TodoContext` helps you interact with the database and commits the changes as a single unit of work. `TodoContext` is configured to use the SQL Server, and the connection string is read from the `config.json` file that we will add in the next step.

3. Add using statement to import `Microsoft.EntityFrameworkCore` in `Startup.cs`.

4. Configure the SQL service by adding the following code snippet to the `ConfigureServices` method:

```
services.AddEntityFrameworkSqlServer()
.AddDbContext<TodoContext>(options =>
options.UseSqlServer(Configuration.GetConnectionString
("DefaultConnection")));
services.AddMvc();
```

5. Add an `appsettings.json` file to hold the value of the connection string and update it with this content:

```
{
  "ConnectionStrings":
  {
    "DefaultConnection": "Server=(localdb)\\mssqllocaldb;
        Database=aspnet-CloudInsights-f2d509d5-468f-4bc9-
        9c47-
        0593d0907063;Trusted_Connection=True;
        MultipleActiveResultSets=true"
  },
  "Logging":
  {
    "IncludeScopes": false,
    "LogLevel": {
     "Default": "Warning"
    }
```

```
        }
    }
```

In this JSON file, we added the connect string under the data item.

Next, we will add and configure Entity Framework in our application. The complete code snippet of the Startup.cs file is as follows:

```
public class Startup
    {
        public Startup(IHostingEnvironment    env)
        {
            var builder = new    ConfigurationBuilder()
                .SetBasePath(env.ContentRootPath)
                .AddJsonFile("appsettings.json",    optional: true,
reloadOnChange: true)
                .AddJsonFile($"appsettings.{env.EnvironmentName}.json",
optional: true)
                .AddEnvironmentVariables();
            Configuration =    builder.Build();
        }
        public IConfigurationRoot    Configuration { get; }
        // This method gets    called by the runtime. Use this method to add
services to the container.
        // For more information    on how to configure your application,
visit    https://go.microsoft.com/fwlink/?LinkID=398940
        public void ConfigureServices(IServiceCollection    services)
        {
            services.AddEntityFrameworkSqlServer()
            .AddDbContext<TodoContext>(options =>
options.UseSqlServer(Configuration.GetConnectionString("DefaultConnection")
));
            // Add framework    services.
            services.AddMvc();
        }
        // This method gets    called by the runtime. Use this method to
configure the HTTP request    pipeline.
        public void    Configure(IApplicationBuilder app,
IHostingEnvironment env, ILoggerFactory    loggerFactory)
        {
            loggerFactory.AddConsole();
            if    (env.IsDevelopment())
            {
                app.UseDeveloperExceptionPage();
            }
            app.UseDefaultFiles();
            app.UseStaticFiles();
            app.UseStaticFiles(new StaticFileOptions
```

```
        {
            FileProvider =    new PhysicalFileProvider(
                Path.Combine(env.ContentRootPath, "node_modules")
            ),
            RequestPath = "/"   + "node_modules"
        });
        app.UseMvc();
    }
}
```

In the `Startup.cs` constructor, we built the configuration to read from the `config.json` file. In the `ConfigureServices` method, we added Entity Framework and hooked the SQL Server and `TodoContext` to it.

Using DB Migration

DB migration in Entity Framework helps you create a database or update a database schema during the application's development phase. We now have the required model and database context in place. We need to create the database now. Let's create the database in SQL Server Compact using the feature called database migration in Entity Framework. Follow these steps to do so:

1. First, add the following XML tags to the `csproj` file by editing it:

```
<ItemGroup>
  <DotNetCliToolReference
  Include="Microsoft.EntityFrameworkCore.Tools.DotNet"
  Version="1.0.0" />
</ItemGroup>
```

2. Open Command Prompt and navigate to the project folder.

3. Execute the following command to initialize the database for migration:

```
C:\Windows\System32\cmd.exe

E:\Packt\My Todo\My Todo>dotnet ef migrations add InitialCreate

Build succeeded.
    0 Warning(s)
    0 Error(s)

Time Elapsed 00:00:03.82
Done. To undo this action, use 'ef migrations remove'

E:\Packt\My Todo\My Todo>
```

Execute the command to add migration

This command creates the `Migration` folder under the **My Todo** project and adds two classes to create tables and update the schema.

Files related to database migration

4. Execute the following command to update the database:

```
E:\Packt\My Todo\My Todo>dotnet ef database update

Build succeeded.
    0 Warning(s)
    0 Error(s)

Time Elapsed 00:00:04.49
Done.

E:\Packt\My Todo\My Todo>
```

Execute the command to update database

This command creates the `database` for our application as per the context and model.

Using Database Context in a Web API controller

Now that we have the database context in place and the migration is also set up, let's update the `TodosController` Web API controller to use `TodoContext` that we created earlier. Follow these steps to do so:

1. Open `TodosController.cs`.
2. Declare the `_db` private variable of the `TodoContext` type:

```
private TodoContext _db;
```

3. Define `constructor` that takes a `context` argument of the `TodoContext` type and assign the `context` value to `_db`:

```
public TodosController(TodoContext context)
{
    _db = context;
}
```

4. Introduce a GET action method that returns the collection of all `Todo` items from the database using the `_db` database context:

```
// GET: api/todos
[HttpGet]
public IEnumerable<Todo> Get()
{
    return _db.Todos.ToList();
}
```

5. Introduce another GET action method that removes the completed `Todo` items from the database and returns all the pending `Todo` items using the `_db` database context:

```
// GET: api/todos/pending-only
[HttpGet]
[Route("pending-only")]
public IEnumerable<Todo> GetPendingOnly()
{
    _db.Todos.RemoveRange(_db.Todos.Where(x =>
    x.Completed == true));
    _db.SaveChanges();
    return _db.Todos.ToList();
}
```

6. Introduce a POST action method that inserts a new Todo item in the TodoContext_db database:

```
// POST api/todos
[HttpPost]
public Todo Post([FromBody]Todo value)
{
    _db.Todos.Add(value);
    _db.SaveChanges();
    return value;
}
```

7. Introduce a PUT action method that updates the existing Todo item that has the matching ID using TodoContext_db:

```
// PUT api/todos/id
[HttpPut("{id}")]
public Todo Put(int id, [FromBody]Todo value)
{
    var todo = _db.Todos.FirstOrDefault(x => x.Id
    == id);
    todo.Title = value.Title;
    todo.Completed = value.Completed;
    _db.Entry(todo).State =
    Microsoft.Data.Entity.EntityState.Modified;
    _db.SaveChanges();
    return value;
}
```

8. Introduce a DELETE action method that deletes an existing Todo item that has the matching ID using TodoContext_db:

```
// DELETE api/todos/id
[HttpDelete("{id}")]
public void Delete(int id)
{
    var todo = _db.Todos.FirstOrDefault(x => x.Id
    == id);
    _db.Entry(todo).State =
    Microsoft.Data.Entity.EntityState.Deleted;
    _db.SaveChanges();
}
```

`TodosController` has methods that are mapped with HTTP verbs, such as GET, POST, PUT, and DELETE. There are two GET actions: one to return all `Todo` items and another to return only the pending `Todo` items, deleting the completed `Todo` items. A POST action that receives a new `Todo` object will insert it into the database using Entity Framework. A PUT action takes two arguments: the `id` of the `Todo` item being updated and the `Todo` object itself. This method first fetches the matching `Todo` item, updates all the properties, and updates the database. Lastly, a DELETE action takes the `id` of the `Todo` item that is to be deleted; it queries the database for the matching `Todo` item and deletes it. The complete code snippet of `TodosController` is this:

```
[Produces("application/json")]
    [Route("api/Todos")]
    public class TodosController   : Controller
    {
        private TodoContext _db;
        public   TodosController(TodoContext context)
        {
            _db = context;
        }
        // GET: api/todos
        [HttpGet]
        public   IEnumerable<Todo> Get()
        {
            return
            _db.Todos.ToList();
        }
        // GET: api/todos/pending-only
        [HttpGet]
        [Route("pending-only")]
        public   IEnumerable<Todo> GetPendingOnly()
        {
            _db.Todos.RemoveRange(_db.Todos.Where(x =>
            x.Completed == true));
            _db.SaveChanges();
            return   _db.Todos.ToList();
        }
        // POST api/todos
        [HttpPost]
        public Todo    Post([FromBody]Todo value)
        {
            _db.Todos.Add(value);
            _db.SaveChanges();
            return value;
        }
        // PUT api/todos/id
        [HttpPut("{id}")]
```

```
public Todo Put(int id,    [FromBody]Todo value)
{
    var todo =   _db.Todos.FirstOrDefault(x =>
    x.Id == id);
    todo.Title =   value.Title;
    todo.Completed =    value.Completed;
    _db.Entry(todo).State    =
    EntityState.Modified;
    _db.SaveChanges();
    return value;
}
// DELETE api/todos/id
[HttpDelete("{id}")]
public void Delete(int    id)
{
    var todo =   _db.Todos.FirstOrDefault(x =>
    x.Id == id);
    _db.Entry(todo).State    = EntityState.Deleted;
    _db.SaveChanges();
}
}
```

Integrating ASP.NET Core Web API with Angular application

In the preceding section, we added and modified the Web API controller and introduced methods for HTTP verbs to deal with the Todo items. Now, let's modify our Angular code to consume all the Web API methods to manage the Todo items.

Updating a model in an Angular app

First, we need to add the id property to Todo.ts in an Angular app to hold the ID of the Todo item received from the API. So, the updated Todo.ts will look as follows:

```
export class Todo {
    id: number;
    title: string;
    completed: boolean;
    constructor(id: number, title: string, completed:
    boolean) {
        this.id = id;
        this.title = title;
```

```
            this.completed = completed;
        }
    set isCompleted(value: boolean) {
            this.completed = value;
        }
    }
}
```

The `constructor` takes three arguments: `id`, `title`, and `completed`, and assigns them to the `id`, `title`, and `completed` properties respectively, accessing them using the `this` keyword. The `Todo` class also sets an accessor for the `completed` property.

Preparing Angular application

The following are the steps for preparing Angular application:

1. Add the `@angular/http` module to dependencies in `package.json`. The HTTP module is required to consume Web API services. The updated `package.json` is given here:

```
{
    "version": "1.0.0",
    "name": "my-todo",
    "private": true,
    "dependencies": {
        "@angular/common": "~4.0.0",
        "@angular/compiler": "~4.0.0",
        "@angular/core": "~4.0.0",
        "@angular/forms": "~4.0.0",
        "@angular/http": "~4.0.0",
        "@angular/platform-browser": "~4.0.0",
        "@angular/platform-browser-dynamic":    "~4.0.0",
        "systemjs": "0.19.40",
        "core-js": "^2.4.1",
        "rxjs": "5.0.1",
        "zone.js": "^0.8.4"
    },
    "devDependencies": {
        "@types/node": "^6.0.46",
        "gulp": "^3.9.1",
        "typescript": "~2.1.0"
    }
}
```

2. Update `systemjs.config.js` with the mapping for `@angular/http`. The updated `systemjs.config.js` is as shown:

```
(function (global) {
    System.config({
        paths: {
            'npm:': 'node_modules/'
        },
        map: {
            'app': 'app',
            '@angular/common':
'npm:@angular/common/bundles/common.umd.js',
            '@angular/compiler':
'npm:@angular/compiler/bundles/compiler.umd.js',
            '@angular/core':
'npm:@angular/core/bundles/core.umd.js',
            '@angular/forms':
'npm:@angular/forms/bundles/forms.umd.js',
            '@angular/http':
'npm:@angular/http/bundles/http.umd.js',
            '@angular/platform-browser':
'npm:@angular/platform-browser/bundles/platform-
  browser.umd.js',
            '@angular/platform-browser-dynamic':
'npm:@angular/platform-browser-
  dynamic/bundles/platform-browser-dynamic.umd.js',
            'rxjs': 'npm:rxjs'
        },
         packages: {
            app: {
                main: './main.js',
                defaultExtension:    'js'
            },
            rxjs: {
                defaultExtension:    'js'
            }
        }
    });
})(this);
```

3. Import the `HttpModule` in `AppModule`, as illustrated:

```
import { NgModule } from '@angular/core';
import { BrowserModule } from '@angular/platform-
browser';
import { FormsModule } from '@angular/forms';
import { HttpModule } from '@angular/http';
```

```
import { AppComponent } from './app.component';
import { TodoService } from './todo.service'
@NgModule({
imports: [
    BrowserModule,
    FormsModule,
    HttpModule
],
    declarations: [AppComponent],
    providers: [TodoService],
    bootstrap: [AppComponent]
})
export class AppModule { }
```

4. Update model Todo, as shown:

```
export class Todo {
    id: number;
    title: string;
    completed: boolean;
    constructor(id: number,   title: string, completed: boolean) {
        this.id = id;
        this.title = title;
        this.completed =   completed;
    }
    set isCompleted(value:   boolean) {
        this.completed = value;
    }
}
```

Consuming Web API GET Action in TodoService

First, let's update the TodoService that consumes Web API service to fetch a list of Todo items. We will use the Http service to communicate with Web API service:

1. Open the todoService.ts file in an app folder.
2. Add the following import statements to import modules such as Injectable, Http, headers, Response, Observable, map, and Todo:

```
import { Injectable } from '@angular/core';
import { Http, Headers } from '@angular/http';
import 'rxjs/add/operator/toPromise';
import { Todo } from './todo'
```

3. Modify `constructor` to inject the `Http` service by adding the parameter for the `Http` service:

```
constructor (private http: Http) { ... }
```

4. Add the `getTodos` method to consume the Web API service to get the list of `Todo` items using the `Http` tag:

```
getTodos(): Promise<Array<Todo>> {
    return this.http.get('/api/todos')
        .toPromise()
        .then(response => response.json() as
        Array<Todo>)
        .catch(this.handleError);
}
```

Here, the `toPromise` method converts the `Observable` sequence returned by the `Get` method of `http`. Then, we call the `then` method or the `catch` method on the returned promise. We convert the JSON received in response into an array of `Todo`.

5. We just added the `getTodos` method. Next, let's add the `getPendingTodos` method to consume the GET method that is configured with the `pending-only` route in the Web API that removes the completed `Todo` items from the database and returns only the pending `Todo` items. The code snippet of `GetPendingTodos` is as follows:

```
getPendingTodos() {
this.http.get('http://localhost:2524/api/todos/
pending-only')
    .subscribe(
    err => console.log(err),
    () => console.log('getTodos Complete')
    );
}
```

Note that we have not updated the `todos` view model in the Angular app with the returned pending `todo` items because we filtered the `Todo` collection in Angular itself to discard the completed `Todo` items, as shown in the following code snippet of `app.component.ts`:

```
getPending() {
return this.todos.filter((todo: Todo) =>
todo.completed === false);
}
```

The updated `todo.service.ts` with the code that consumes both the GET methods of the Web API is as follows:

```
import { Injectable } from '@angular/core';
import { Http, Headers } from '@angular/http';
import 'rxjs/add/operator/toPromise';
import { Todo } from './todo'
@Injectable()
export class TodoService {
    constructor(private http: Http) {    }
    getTodos(): Promise<Array<Todo>> {
        return this.http.get('/api/todos')
            .toPromise()
            .then(response => response.json() as Array<Todo>)
            .catch(this.handleError);
    }
    getPendingTodos() {
        this.http.get('/api/todos/pending-only')
            .subscribe(
            err => console.log(err),
            () => console.log('getTodos Complete')
            );
    }
    removeCompleted() {
        this.getPendingTodos();
    }
    private handleError(error: any): Promise<any> {
        console.error('An error occurred', error);
        return Promise.reject(error.message || error);
    }
}
```

Posting to the Web API from TodoService

We just updated `todo.Services.ts` to call the Web API's GET action and fetch Todo items. Now, let's add code to post a new Todo item to the Web API. Follow the given steps to do so:

1. Open `todo.service.ts`.

2. Add the `postTodo` function that posts a new `Todo` item to the Web API controller:

```
postTodo(todo: Todo): Promise<Todo> {
        var headers = new Headers();
        headers.append('Content-Type',
'application/json');
    return this.http.post('/api/todos',
JSON.stringify(todo), { headers: headers })
        .toPromise()
        .then(response => response.json() as Todo)
        .catch(this.handleError);
}
```

This function accepts a `Todo` item as an argument. It defines the `header` section with the JSON content type and posts the `Todo` item using the `http` service to a Web API asynchronously. The response is converted to `Promise` and the `then` method returns a `Promise<Todo>`.

Calling the PUT action of the Web API to update a Todo item

We just added code to consume the Web API GET action and also added code to POST a new `Todo` item to the Web API. Now, let's consume the PUT action in the Web API to update an existing Todo item. Follow these steps to do so:

1. Open `todo.service.ts`.
2. Add the `putTodo` function with the following code snippet to update the existing `Todo` item by calling the PUT action in the Web API:

```
putTodo(todo: Todo) {
  var headers = new Headers();
  headers.append('Content-Type', 'application/json');
  this.http.put('/api/todos/' + todo.id,
JSON.stringify(todo), { headers: headers })
        .toPromise()
        .then(() => todo)
        .catch(this.handleError);
}
```

This code defines the header with the JSON content type and calls the PUT action method along with the JSON stringified Todo item and the id of that Todo item. The Web API's PUT action method will update the matching Todo item in the database.

Calling the DELETE action of the Web API to delete a Todo item

We added code to get, add, and edit a Todo item by calling various Web API actions, such as GET, POST, and PUT, respectively. Now, let's consume the DELETE action in the Web API to delete a matching Todo item. Follow the given steps to do so:

1. Open todo.service.ts.
2. Add the deleteTodo function with the following code snippet to delete a matching Todo item by calling the DELETE action in the Web API:

```
deleteTodo(todo: Todo) {
  this.http.delete('/api/todos/' + todo.id)
      .subscribe(err => console.log(err),
      () => console.log('getTodos Complete')
      );
  }
```

This code calls the DELETE action along with the id of the Todo item being deleted. The Web API's DELETE action method will retrieve the matching Todo item from the database and delete it.

Updating the wrapper functions in TodoService

We have functions such as getTodos, getPendingTodos, postTodos, putTodo, and deleteTodo that interact with the GET, POST, PUT, and DELETE Web API actions respectively. Now, let's update or replace the code of the remove, add, toggleCompletion, and removeCompleted functions that serve as wrappers that will be consumed from app.component.ts. Update or replace the code of the functions, as shown in the following code snippet:

```
remove(todo: Todo) {
    this.deleteTodo(todo);
}
add(title: string): Promise<Todo> {
    var todo = new Todo(0, title, false);
```

```
        return this.postTodo(todo);
    }
    toggleCompletion(todo: Todo) {
        todo.completed = !todo.completed;
        this.putTodo(todo);
    }
    removeCompleted() {
        this.getPendingTodos();
    }
```

The complete code snippet of `todo.service.ts` after all the updates is this:

```
import { Injectable } from '@angular/core';
import { Http, Headers } from '@angular/http';
import 'rxjs/add/operator/toPromise';
import { Todo } from './todo'
@Injectable()
export class TodoService {
    constructor(private http: Http) {     }
    getTodos(): Promise<Array<Todo>> {
        return this.http.get('/api/todos')
            .toPromise()
            .then(response => response.json() as Array<Todo>)
            .catch(this.handleError);
    }
    getPendingTodos() {
        this.http.get('/api/todos/pending-only')
            .subscribe(
            err => console.log(err),
            () => console.log('getTodos Complete')
            );
    }
    postTodo(todo: Todo): Promise<Todo> {
        var headers = new Headers();
        headers.append('Content-Type', 'application/json');
        return this.http.post('/api/todos', JSON.stringify(todo), {
headers: headers })
            .toPromise()
            .then(response => response.json() as Todo)
            .catch(this.handleError);
    }
    putTodo(todo: Todo) {
        var headers = new Headers();
        headers.append('Content-Type', 'application/json');
        this.http.put('/api/todos/' + todo.id, JSON.stringify(todo), {
headers: headers })
            .toPromise()
            .then(() => todo)
```

```
            .catch(this.handleError);
    }
    deleteTodo(todo: Todo) {
        this.http.delete('/api/todos/' + todo.id)
            .subscribe(err => console.log(err),
            () => console.log('getTodos Complete')
            );
    }
    remove(todo: Todo) {
        this.deleteTodo(todo);
    }
    add(title: string): Promise<Todo> {
        var todo = new Todo(0, title, false);
        return this.postTodo(todo);
    }
    toggleCompletion(todo: Todo) {
        todo.completed = !todo.completed;
        this.putTodo(todo);
    }
    removeCompleted() {
        this.getPendingTodos();
    }
    private handleError(error: any): Promise<any> {
        console.error('An error occurred', error);
        return Promise.reject(error.message || error);
    }
}
```

Updating AppComponent

We have the updated `todo.service.ts` that interacts with the Web API and is ready for us to consume in `app.component.ts`. The updated code snippet of `app.component.ts` is as shown:

```
import { Component, OnInit } from '@angular/core';
import { Todo } from './todo'
import { TodoService } from './todo.service'
@Component({
    selector: 'my-app',
    templateUrl: './app/app.component.html',
    providers: [TodoService]
})
export class AppComponent implements OnInit {
    todos: Array<Todo>;
    newTodoText = '';
    constructor(private todoService: TodoService) {
```

```
        this.todos = new Array();
    }
    getTodos(): void {
        this.todoService
            .getTodos()
            .then(todos => this.todos = todos);
    }
    ngOnInit(): void {
        this.getTodos();
    }
    removeCompleted() {
        this.todoService.removeCompleted();
        this.todos = this.getPending();
    }
    toggleCompletion(todo: Todo) {
        this.todoService.toggleCompletion(todo);
    }
    remove(todo: Todo) {
        this.todoService.remove(todo);
        this.todos.splice(this.todos.indexOf(todo), 1);
    }
    addTodo() {
        if (this.newTodoText.trim().length) {
        this.todoService.add(this.newTodoText).then(res =>
{
            this.getTodos();
            });
            this.newTodoText = '';
            this.getTodos();
        }
    }
    getPending() {
        return this.todos.filter((todo: Todo) => todo.completed === false);
    }
    getCompleted() {
        return this.todos.filter((todo: Todo) => todo.completed === true);
    }
}
```

Updating the AppComponent template

The updated content of `app.component.html` is as illustrated in the following code snippet:

```html
<section>
    <header>
        <h1>todos</h1>
        <input placeholder="Add new todo" autofocus=""
[(ngModel)]="newTodoText">
        <button type="button" (click)="addTodo()">Add</button>
    </header>
    <section>
        <ul>
            <li *ngFor="let todo of todos">
                <input type="checkbox" (click)="toggleCompletion(todo)"
[checked]="todo.completed">
                <label>{{todo.title}}</label>
                <button (click)="remove(todo)">X</button>
            </li>
        </ul>
    </section>
    <footer *ngIf="todos.length > 0">
        <span><strong>{{getPending().length}}</strong>
{{getPending().length == 1 ? 'item' : 'items'}} left</span>
        <button *ngIf="getCompleted().length > 0"
(click)="removeCompleted()">Clear completed</button>
    </footer>
</section>
```

The `TexBox` input is applied with two-way binding using `ngModel` to bind the new `Todo` item, `title`. The `Add` button-click event is wired up with the `addTodo` method in `AppComponent`. The available `Todo` items will be listed in the `<li>` tag using `ngFor` that iterates each `Todo` item in `TodoService`. The checkbox rendered for each `Todo` item has its `click` event and the `checked` property mapped with the `toggleCompletion` method and a `completed` property of the `Todo` item, respectively. Next, the remove button has its `click` event mapped with the `remove` method in `AppComponent`.

The footer tag has a span that displays the pending Todo items' count and a button to remove the completed Todo items from the list. This button has a click event mapped with the removeCompleted method in AppComponent.

Updating the index page

There is no change in the index page template. The following code snippet has the full content of index.html:

```html
<!DOCTYPE html>
<html>
<head>
    <title>My Todo</title>
    <script>document.write('<base href="' +
    document.location + '" />');</script>
    <meta charset="UTF-8">
    <!-- Polyfills -->
    <script src="libs/shim.min.js"></script>
    <script src="libs/zone.min.js"></script>
    <script src="libs/system.src.js"></script>
    <script src="systemjs.config.js"></script>
    <script>
      System.import('main.js').catch(function(err){ console.error(err); });
    </script>
</head>
<body>
    <my-app>Loading My Todo App...</my-app>
</body>
</html>
```

Note that the body tag has a special <my-app/> tag, which is the metadata in AppComponent. This is where AppComponent will be instantiated and rendered using the template.

Running the application

Let's run the application by pressing *F5*, and after this, you will be able to perform operations such as adding, editing, removing, and listing `Todo` items:

My Todo App with all the operations

Summary

We started this chapter with an introduction to RESTful services and gave you an overview of the ASP.NET Web API. We also discussed why the ASP.NET Web API is the best fit for Angular applications. Then, you learned about adding and configuring Entity Framework in an ASP.NET 5 project and the steps required to create a database using database migration. Next, we walked through the process of creating a Web API service and managing data using Entity Framework. Finally, you learned about consuming the Web API from Angular applications.

In this chapter, we discussed how to consume a Web API service from an Angular application to add, update, delete, and retrieve the Todo items from a database using Entity Framework.

In the next chapter, we will discuss how to integrate an Angular application with the ASP.NET MVC and Web API.

7

Creating an Application Using Angular, ASP.NET MVC, and Web API in Visual Studio

This chapter guides you through the process of integrating an Angular application with ASP.NET MVC and the ASP.NET Web API. In the last chapter, we consumed ASP.NET Web API services using Angular applications. All the views are rendered by Angular. In this chapter, we will serve the views from ASP.NET MVC. So, it opens lots of opportunities, such as using Razor syntax, as the Angular view will be powered by ASP.NET MVC.

In this chapter, we will cover the following topics:

- Using ASP.NET MVC to serve views for Angular component templates
- Combining routing for ASP.NET MVC, the ASP.NET Web API, and Angular

Using ASP.NET MVC

ASP.NET includes web stacks such as ASP.NET MVC, Razor, and Web APIs. The ASP.NET MVC framework was built on top of ASP.NET. The ASP.NET MVC web framework implements the **Model-View-Controller (MVC)** pattern to develop web applications.

In the MVC pattern, **Model** represents the state of the business object. **View** represents the user interface and **Controller** handles the communication between the model and view. All requests will be handled by controllers and a response will be returned:

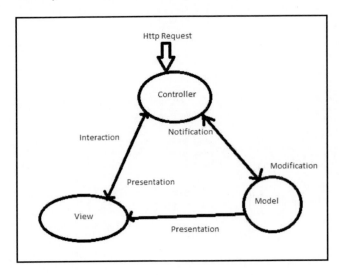

The MVC architecture

ASP.NET MVC has its own view engine called the Razor engine.

Combining routing for ASP.NET MVC, the ASP.NET Web API, and Angular

Routing is the process of decomposing an endpoint to identify a module or controller and action that can handle a request. Routing makes the URL readable and meaningful. It also helps in hiding data from users.

Routing in ASP.NET MVC

ASP.NET MVC routing maps the request to the controller actions. All routes will be defined in the route table and are used by the route engine to match the URL patterns of the requests with the controllers and actions.

We can add the routes to the route table in the configure method of the `Startup.cs` file. The following code snippet shows the default route registered on the route table:

```
public void Configure(IApplicationBuilder app)
{
    app.UseIISPlatformHandler();
    app.UseDefaultFiles();
    app.UseStaticFiles();
    app.UseMvc(config =>
    {
        config.MapRoute(
            name: "Default",
            template: "{controller}/{action}/{id?}",
            defaults: new { controller = "Home", action = "Index" }
            );
    });
}
```

Here, a route is registered with a template and defaults. If there is no controller or action name provided in the URL, the request will be mapped to the `Index` action in the `HomeController` class; otherwise, it will be mapped to the respective controller action.

In our application, we have three MVC controllers, namely, `HomeController`, `UserController`, and `TodoController`.

Adding ASP.NET MVC HomeController

This controller has a single action called `Index` that returns the `Index` view as a response. The following is the code snippet of the `Index` action:

```
public IActionResult Index()
{
    return View();
}
```

When a request is routed to the `Index` action, it will return the `Index` view. The source code of `Index.cshtml` is as shown in the following code snippet:

```
@{
    Layout = null;
}
<!DOCTYPE html>
<html>
<head>
    <meta name="viewport" content="width=device-width" />
    <title>Index</title>
```

```
</head>
<body>
    <h1>index view</h1>
</body>
</html>
```

Follow the given steps to add the ASP.NET MVC `HomeController` and its corresponding view to our `My Todo` application created in the earlier chapters:

1. Right-click on the `Controllers` folder and add a new controller.
2. Name the newly added controller as `HomeController`. Note that there is an `Index` action added to `HomeController` by default.
3. Now, let's add a view for the `Index` action. Right-click on the `My Todo` application and add a new folder named `Views`.
4. Then, add a folder named `Home` under the `Views` folder we just created.
5. Right-click on the `Home` folder and add a new view named `Index.cshtml`:

ASP.NET MVC HomeController Index View

Routing for ASP.NET MVC

We just created an ASP.NET MVC controller and added a view for an Index action in the controller. Now we need to configure routing for the ASP.NET MVC application so that any request to the Index action is handled by the ASP.NET MVC router. Follow these steps to configure ASP.NET MVC routing:

1. Open Startup.cs.
2. Comment or remove the app.UseDefaultFiles() statement from the Configure method as we will serve views using ASP.NET MVC.
3. Replace the app.UseMvc() statement in the Configure method with this one:

```
app.UseMvc(config =>
    {
       config.MapRoute(
       name: "Default",
       template: "{controller}/{action}/{id?}",
defaults: new    { controller = "Home", action =
"Index" }
        );
    });
```

Here, we have added the default routing for ASP.NET MVC. Any request to the Web API is mapped with the HTTP verbs or actions in the controller.

Let's run the application by pressing *F5*, and you will get the illustrated screen rendered in the browser:

ASP.NET MVC HomeController Index View rendered in browser

Moving the content from the default page to the ASP.NET MVC view

In the preceding section, we were able to run the application and noticed that the default view is served is the ASP.NET MVC Index view of HomeController. Now, let's update the Index.cshtml view with the content of the Index.html file located under the wwwroot folder. The updated Index.cshtml is shown here:

```
@{
    Layout = null;
}
<!DOCTYPE html>
<html>
<head>
    <title>My    Todo</title>
    <script>document.write('<base    href="' +
    document.location + '" />');</script>
    <meta charset="UTF-8">
    <!-- Polyfills -->
    <script src="libs/shim.min.js"></script>
    <script src="libs/zone.min.js"></script>
    <script src="libs/system.src.js"></script>
    <script src="systemjs.config.js"></script>
    <script>
    System.import('main.js').catch(function(err){
    console.error(err); });
    </script>
</head>
<body>
    <h1>My Todo    App</h1>
    <my-app>Loading My Todo    App...</my-app>
</body>
</html>
```

Run the application now by pressing *F5* and note that the `my-app` special tag has been replaced with the parsed template of `app.component.html` by Angular, as follows:

Angular app loaded onto the ASP.NET MVC Index view

Routing in the ASP.NET Web API

Any request to the Web API is mapped with the HTTP verbs or actions in the controller using routing. Web API 2 introduced an attribute-based routing technique called **attribute routing**. Attribute routing can be added at the controller level and action level. We can decorate a Web API controller with a `Route` attribute by passing the template of the URL, as demonstrated in the following code snippet:

```
[Route("api/[controller]")]
public class TodosController : Controller
{
    // GET: api/todos/pending-only
    [HttpGet]
    [Route("pending-only")]
    public IEnumerable<Todo> GetPendingOnly()
    {
    }
}
```

Here, `TodosController` is decorated by Route with the `api/[controller]` URL template. This means that if the request is received with `http://www.programmerguide.net/api/todos`, it will be routed to `TodosController`, and the action will be selected based on the HTTP action applied.

Note that the GetPendingOnly action is decorated by Route with the pending-only URL template. This means that if there are more GET actions available in the controller and if the request URL is http://www.programmerguide.net/api/todos/pending-only, it will be mapped to the GetPendingOnly action.

The complete source code of the TodosController Web API controller is as follows:

```
[Produces("application/json")]
    [Route("api/Todos")]
    public class TodosController : Controller
    {
        private TodoContext _db;
        public TodosController(TodoContext context)
        {
            _db = context;
        }
        // GET: api/todos
        [HttpGet]
        public IEnumerable<Todo> Get()
        {
            return _db.Todos.ToList();
        }
        // GET: api/todos/pending-only
        [HttpGet]
        [Route("pending-only")]
        public IEnumerable<Todo> GetPendingOnly()
        {
            _db.Todos.RemoveRange(_db.Todos.Where(x =>
            x.Completed == true));
            _db.SaveChanges();
            return _db.Todos.ToList();
        }
        // POST api/todos
        [HttpPost]
        public Todo Post([FromBody]Todo value)
        {
            _db.Todos.Add(value);
            _db.SaveChanges();
            return value;
        }
        // PUT api/todos/id
        [HttpPut("{id}")]
        public Todo Put(int id, [FromBody]Todo value)
        {
            var todo = _db.Todos.FirstOrDefault(x => x.Id
            == id);
            todo.Title = value.Title;
```

```
            todo.Completed = value.Completed;
            _db.Entry(todo).State = EntityState.Modified;
            _db.SaveChanges();
            return value;
    }
    // DELETE api/todos/id
    [HttpDelete("{id}")]
    public void Delete(int id)
    {
            var todo = _db.Todos.FirstOrDefault(x => x.Id
            == id);
            _db.Entry(todo).State = EntityState.Deleted;
            _db.SaveChanges();
    }
}
```

Routing in Angular

As we saw in `Chapter 3`, *Angular Building Blocks - Part 2*, Angular introduced a component router that deep links the URL request, maps the component that is annotated for this route, and renders the template or view associated with the component. The Angular router is not part of the core Angular framework. It comes as part of the Angular router module. We need to add the reference to this library in `package.json`, as follows, under the dependencies section:

```
"dependencies": {
"@angular/router": "~4.0.0",
}
```

Then, we need to add the <base> element under <head> to instruct the router to set up navigation URLs. The following code snippet shows the <base> tag with the `href` attribute that should be added to the `head` tag in the `index` file, considering that the app folder is the root of the application:

```
<base href="/">
```

The router decides the component and template by looking at `RouteDefinition` for the URL requested by the browser. So, we need to configure the route definitions.

We will have three hyperlinks on the index page, namely `todo`, `about`, and `contact`. Clicking on `todo` will navigate the user to the `todo` app, clicking on `about` will navigate to `about` view, and finally, clicking on `contact` will navigate the user to the `contact` view. So, we need to add two more components, namely `AboutComponent` and `ContactComponent`, and their respective template files, namely `about.component.html` and `contact.component.html` respectively. Follow the mentioned steps to create these components and their templates:

1. Right-click on the `app` folder and add two HTML templates: `about.component.html` and `contact.component.html`.

2. Add the following HTML snippet as the content of `about.component.html`:

```
<h1>This is the About    View</h1>
```

3. Add this HTML snippet as the content of `contact.component.html`:

```
<h1>This is the Contact    View</h1>
```

4. Right-click on the `app` folder and add two Angular components: `about.component.ts` and `contact.component.ts`.

5. Add the following code snippet to `about.component.ts`:

```
import { Component } from '@angular/core';
@Component({
    selector: 'about-me',
    templateUrl: './app/about.component.html',
})
export class AboutComponent { }
```

6. Add the next code snippet to `contact.component.ts`:

```
import { Component } from '@angular/core';
@Component({
    selector: 'contact-us',
    templateUrl: './app/contact.component.html',
})
   export class ContactComponent { }
```

7. Let's also create an Angular component, `todo.component.ts`, and move the properties and methods in `app.component.ts` to `todo.component.ts`. Also, update the import and annotations of `TodoComponent`. The complete code snippet of `TodoComponent` is as shown:

```
import { Component, OnInit } from    '@angular/core';
import { Todo } from './todo'
import { TodoService } from './todo.service'
@Component({
    selector: 'my-app',
    templateUrl: './app/todo.component.html',
    providers: [TodoService]
})
  export class TodoComponent    implements OnInit {
    todos: Array<Todo>;
    newTodoText = '';
  constructor(private   todoService: TodoService) {
    this.todos = new Array();
  }
    getTodos(): void {
      this.todoService
      .getTodos()
      .then(todos =>   this.todos = todos);
  }
  ngOnInit(): void {
   this.getTodos();
  }
   removeCompleted() {
   this.todoService.removeCompleted();
   this.todos =    this.getPending();
  }
  toggleCompletion(todo: Todo)    {
     this.todoService.toggleCompletion(todo);
  }
  remove(todo: Todo) {
     this.todoService.remove(todo);
     this.todos.splice(this.todos.indexOf(todo), 1);
  }
  addTodo() {
     if (this.newTodoText.trim().length)    {
     this.todoService.add(this.newTodoText).then(res
     => {
     this.getTodos();
     });
     this.newTodoText = '';
     this.getTodos();
     }
```

```
    }
    getPending() {
        return this.todos.filter((todo:    Todo) =>
 todo.completed === false);
    }
    getCompleted() {
    return   this.todos.filter((todo: Todo) =>
    todo.completed === true);
    }
 }
```

8. Now, create the `todo.component.html` template and move the content of `app.component.html`. The updated `todo.component.html` is as illustrated:

```html
<section>
    <header>
        <h1>todos</h1>
        <input placeholder="Add   new todo" autofocus=""
        [(ngModel)]="newTodoText">
        <button type="button"
        (click)="addTodo()">Add</button>
    </header>
<section>
    <ul>
        <li *ngFor="let   todo of todos">
        <input type="checkbox"
        (click)="toggleCompletion(todo)"
        [checked]="todo.completed">
        <label>{{todo.title}}</label>
        <button    (click)="remove(todo)">X</button>
        </li>
    </ul>
</section>
        <footer *ngIf="todos.length    > 0">
        <span><strong>{{getPending().length}}</strong>
        {{getPending().length == 1 ? 'item' : 'items'}}
        left</span>
        <button *ngIf="getCompleted().length   > 0"
        (click)="removeCompleted()">Clear
        completed</button>
        </footer>
</section>
```

9. Next, add a `app.routing.ts` file and update it with the following code snippet. Here, we configured three routings for `todo`, `about`, and `contact` respectively. Also, we assigned three components--TodoComponent, AboutComponent and ContactComponent--to export the metadata of the `NgModule` attribute:

```
import { NgModule } from '@angular/core';
import { Routes, RouterModule }   from
'@angular/router';
import { TodoComponent } from './todo.component';
import { AboutComponent } from './about.component';
import { ContactComponent } from
'./contact.component';
export const appRoutes: Routes =   [
    {
        path: '',
        redirectTo: 'todo',
        pathMatch: 'full',
    },
    { path: 'todo', component:   TodoComponent, data:
      { title: 'Todo' } },
    { path: 'about', component:  AboutComponent, data:
      { title: 'About' } },
    { path: 'contact', component: ContactComponent,
      data: { title: 'Contact' } }
];
export const routedComponents = [
    TodoComponent,
    AboutComponent,
    ContactComponent
];
@NgModule({
    imports:    [RouterModule.forRoot(appRoutes)],
    exports: [RouterModule]
})
  export class AppRoutingModule { }
```

10. Update `app.module.ts` as follows to import `AppRoutingModule` that we created in the last step:

```
import { NgModule } from '@angular/core';
import { BrowserModule } from '@angular/platform-
browser';
import { FormsModule } from '@angular/forms';
import { HttpModule } from '@angular/http';
import { AppComponent } from './app.component';
import { TodoComponent } from './todo.component';
import { AboutComponent } from './about.component';
```

```
import { ContactComponent } from
'./contact.component';
import { AppRoutingModule } from './app.routing';
import { TodoService } from './todo.service'
@NgModule({
    imports: [
        BrowserModule,
        FormsModule,
        HttpModule,
        AppRoutingModule
    ],
    declarations: [
        AppComponent,
        TodoComponent,
        AboutComponent,
        ContactComponent
    ],
    providers: [TodoService],
    bootstrap: [AppComponent]
})
export class AppModule { }
```

11. Finally, update the `app.component.html` as follows:

```
<a routerLinkActive="active"   [routerLink]="
['/todo']">Todo</a>
<a routerLinkActive="active"   [routerLink]="
['/about']">About</a>
<a routerLinkActive="active"   [routerLink]="
['/contact']">Contact</a>
<router-outlet></router-outlet>
```

Note that each hyperlink has the `routerLink` attribute and is assigned with the route path. Here, the `routerLinkActive` attribute is assigned with the `active` CSS class, which will be added to the element when this route becomes active. In other words, when the user clicks on the `Todo` link, that link gets the `active` CSS class assigned to it.

The `routerLink` attribute enables the application to link to a specific part or component of the application. The next statement is the `<router-outlet/>` special tag for the component router, which is similar to the `<ng-view/>` tag in AngularJS 1.x in that it is used to load the templates associated with the corresponding path of the route.

12. Run the application by pressing *F5*, and the browser will load the application by navigating to the **Todo** route as we have set up a redirect to `todo` if it is a root path:

The todo template is loaded and the URL has the \todo path

13. Clicking on the **About** link will navigate to the `\about` path, and the parsed template view of `about` will be loaded:

The about template is loaded and the URL has the \about path

14. Clicking on the **Contact** link will navigate to the \contact path, and the parsed template view of about will be loaded:

The contact template is loaded and the URL has the \contact path

Notice the address bar for the changes in route path in the URL.

Moving the Angular template to the ASP.NET MVC template

We have almost completed the application. However, we have only used Angular views as templates for the Angular components. We need to serve the template via ASP.NET MVC. This will enable us to add Razor codes, if necessary, as these views are powered by ASP.NET MVC. Follow the given steps to add Razor views and update the templateUrl in each Angular component:

1. First, add three actions in HomeController, namely About, Contact, and Todo, as follows:

```
public IActionResult    About()
{
    return View();
}
public IActionResult    Contact()
{
    return View();
}
public IActionResult    Todo()
{
    return View();
}
```

2. Add three views, namely `About`, `Contact`, and `Todo`, under the `Views` -> `Home` folder, as shown:

Razor views added under Home

3. Add this HTML content to `About.cshtml`:

```
<h1>This is the About Razor   View</h1>
```

4. Add the following HTML content to `Contact.cshtml`:

```
<h1>This is the Contact Razor View</h1>
```

5. Then, move the content of `todo.component.html` to `Todo.cshtml`:

6. Now we need to update the metadata of the `templateUrl` of `AboutComponent`, `ContactComponent`, and `TodoComponent` with the URLs of the respective actions in HomeController:

```
TodoComponent:
      templateUrl: '/Home/Todo'
AboutComponent:
      templateUrl: '/Home/About'
ContactComponent:
      templateUrl: '/Home/Contact',
```

7. Now, run the application by pression *F5* and note that the views are served from ASP.NET MVC. You can add Razor syntax as well to the views as they are now powered by ASP.NET MVC.

8. Clicking on the About link will navigate to the \about path and instantiate the matching component. Here, it is AboutComponent and the appropriate Razor view of about will be rendered:

The About Razor template rendered

9. Clicking on the **Contact** link will navigate to the \contact path and initiate the ContactComponent, which is responsible for rendering the Contact Razor view:

The Contact Razor template rendered

A click on logout will redirect you to the login view.

Summary

Hurray! We just created an Angular application powered by ASP.NET MVC with the backend Web API. We combined the routing of Angular and ASP.NET MVC and demonstrated how these routings are connected to each other.

In the next chapter, we will discuss the testing of an Angular application.

8

Testing Angular Applications

This chapter discusses testing Angular components and services using the Jasmine framework.

In this chapter, we will cover the following topics:

- Introducing Jasmine
- Testing Angular services
- Testing Angular components

Introducing Jasmine

Jasmine is an open source framework that is used to test JavaScript code without any dependency on DOM. As Angular is loosely coupled, we can use the Jasmine framework to test Angular components, services, and so on. Independent of each other, the clean syntax of Jasmine enables you to write tests very easily.

A global function named describe is the starting point of the Jasmine function. This global function takes a function and two parameters of type string. The string parameter describes the tests, and the function will have the actual implementation of testing:

```
describe("short description about the test suite", function() {
});
```

The actual test methods are defined by a global function called the `it` function, which takes two arguments. The first argument is the title of the test or spec, and the second argument is the function that tests the expectations by verifying the state of the code. Expectations are similar to assert in the Microsoft unit test framework. If any one of the defined expectations fails in the spec, it is called the failing spec. The following code illustrates the preceding statements:

```
describe("short description about the test suite", function() {
  it("a spec with single expectation", function() {
    expect(true).toBe(true);
  });
});
```

The test or spec method will have one or more expect statements, as illustrated, that compare the actual value with the expected value using the matcher functions that are chained to the expect function; various default matcher functions are available:

```
describe("short description about the test suite", function() {
it("a spec with single expectation", function() {
expect(afunction).toThrow(e);
expect(true).toBe(true);
expect(variable).toBeDefined();
expect(variable).toBeFalsy();
expect(number).toBeGreaterThan(number);
expect(number).toBeLessThan(number);
expect(variable).toBeNull();
expect(variable).toBeTruthy();
expect(value).toBeUndefined();
expect(array).toContain(member);
expect(string).toContain(substring);
expect(variable).toEqual(variable);
expect(value).toMatch(pattern);
  });
});
```

We have only seen the basics of the Jasmine framework, and there are more features available. You can learn about them by visiting the official website at `http://jasmine.github.io/`. This introduction is enough for us to learn to test Angular services and components.

Testing Angular services

Let's first create a `Todo.ts` model class that represents the `Todo` item. The following code snippet shows the content of the `Todo` class:

```
export class Todo {
    title: string;
    completed: boolean;
    constructor(title: string) {
        this.title = title;
        this.completed = false;
    }
    set isCompleted(value: boolean) {
        this.completed = value;
    }
}
```

Next, create a service `todo.service.ts` that constructs the list of `Todo` items in the constructor. The complete code of `todo.service.ts` is as shown:

```
import { Todo } from './todo'
export class TodoService {
    todos: Array<Todo>
    constructor() {
        this.todos = [new Todo('First item'),
        new Todo('Second item'),
        new Todo('Third item')];
    }
    getPending() {
        return this.todos.filter((todo: Todo) => todo.completed ===
        false);
    }
    getCompleted() {
        return this.todos.filter((todo: Todo) => todo.completed ===
        true);
    }
    remove(todo: Todo) {
        this.todos.splice(this.todos.indexOf(todo), 1);
    }
    add(title: string) {
        this.todos.push(new Todo(title));
    }
    toggleCompletion(todo: Todo) {
        todo.completed = !todo.completed;
    }
```

```
    removeCompleted() {
        this.todos = this.getPending();
    }
}
```

We have the service that interacts with the data source in place. Now, let's write tests using the Jasmine framework to test the `TodoService`. We will test two methods, namely `getPending()` and `getCompleted()`. Create a file named `todo.service.spec.ts`.

Import the `TodoService` application-specific service, as follows:

```
import { TodoService } from "./todo.service";
```

Define the `describe` method: a global function that is the starting point of the Jasmine function that takes two parameters, a string that describes the tests and a function that has the actual implementation of testing:

```
describe("TodoService Testing",() => {
});
```

Declare the `beforeEach` function that will be executed before running each test inside the `describe` global function. The code snippet of the `describe` function with `beforeEach` is given here:

```
describe('TodoService Testing', () => {
  let service: TodoService;
  beforeEach(() => { service = new TodoService(); });
});
```

The `beforeEach` function will be executed before running each test method, and it serves an instance of `TodoService` for each test.

Now, let's define the `it` test methods, as demonstrated:

```
it('getPending length should return 3', () => {
    expect(service.getPending().length).toBe(3);
});
it('getCompleted length should return 0', () => {
    expect(service.getCompleted().length).toBe(0);
});
```

Here, we are verifying that the expectations of the length of the returned values of `getPending()` and `getCompleted()` match.

The complete code snippet of `todo.service.spec.ts` is this:

```
import { TodoService } from "./todo.service";
describe('TodoService Testing', () => {
  let service: TodoService;
  beforeEach(() => { service = new TodoService(); });
  it('getPending length should return 3', () => {
    expect(service.getPending().length).toBe(3);
  });
  it('getCompleted length should return 0', () => {
    expect(service.getCompleted().length).toBe(0);
  });
});
```

We have the spec or tests ready to run; let's run them by executing the following commands:

```
npm run build:watch
karma start karma.conf.js
```

The `npm run build:watch` command will build your application and transpile the TypeScript files into JavaScript. Then, the `karma start karma.config` command is executed to start the test runner for our application.

Karma is a test runner that can be used to run tests for any JavaScript application. The `karma.config.js` file is a configuration file for karma that provides information about our application to karma in order for it to understand and test the application. The karma configuration file has details of the path of JavaScript libraries and frameworks that the application is consuming, and also, it provides details about the plugins used by karma.

Karma config file has the configuration details for basePath, frameworks, plugins, client, and custom launcher in our application. We have configured Jasmine as our test framework in karma, we have added the list of required modules under plugins to load when running the test. We also configured the client with `buildPaths` and `clearContext`. The `buildPaths` will have path details to look for the transpiled app JS and map files. The following is the complete karma configuration file for your reference:

```
module.exports = function(config)    {
  var appBase    = 'src/';           // transpiled app JS and map files
  var appAssets  = '/base/app/';     // component assets fetched by
  Angular's compiler
  // Testing helpers (optional)    are conventionally in a folder called
      `testing`
  var testingBase    = 'src/testing/';   // transpiled test JS and map
  files
  var testingSrcBase = 'src/testing/';   // test source TS
```

```
  files
config.set({
  basePath: '',
  frameworks: ['jasmine'],
  plugins: [
    require('karma-jasmine'),
    require('karma-chrome-launcher'),
    require('karma-jasmine-html-reporter')
  ],
  client:
{
    builtPaths: [appBase,   testingBase], // add more
    spec base paths
    as needed
    clearContext: false //   leave Jasmine Spec Runner
    output visible
    in browser
  },
  customLaunchers: {
    // From the CLI. Not used   here but interesting
    // chrome setup for travis   CI using chromium
    Chrome_travis_ci: {
      base: 'Chrome',
      flags: ['--no-sandbox']
    }
  },
  files: [
    // System.js for module    loading
    'node_modules/systemjs/dist/system.src.js',
    // Polyfills
    'node_modules/core-js/client/shim.js',
    // zone.js
    'node_modules/zone.js/dist/zone.js',
    'node_modules/zone.js/dist/long-stack-trace-
     zone.js',
    'node_modules/zone.js/dist/proxy.js',
    'node_modules/zone.js/dist/sync-test.js',
    'node_modules/zone.js/dist/jasmine-patch.js',
    'node_modules/zone.js/dist/async-test.js',
    'node_modules/zone.js/dist/fake-async-test.js',
    // RxJs
    { pattern: 'node_modules/rxjs/**/*.js',   included:
      false,
      watched: false },
    { pattern: 'node_modules/rxjs/**/*.js.map',
      included: false,
      watched: false },
    // Paths loaded via module   imports:
```

```
    // Angular itself
    { pattern: 'node_modules/@angular/**/*.js',
      included: false,
      watched: false },
    { pattern: 'node_modules/@angular/**/*.js.map',
      included:
      false, watched: false },
    { pattern: appBase + '/systemjs.config.js',
      included: false,
       watched: false },
    { pattern: appBase + '/systemjs.config.extras.js',
      included:
      false, watched: false },
    'karma-test-shim.js', //    optionally extend
     SystemJS mapping
     e.g., with barrels
    // transpiled application   & spec code paths loaded
       via module
        imports
    { pattern: appBase + '**/*.js',    included: false,
      watched: true
},
    { pattern: testingBase + '**/*.js',    included:
      false, watched:
      true
},
    // Asset (HTML & CSS)    paths loaded via Angular's
       component
       compiler
    // (these paths need to be    rewritten, see proxies
        section)
    { pattern: appBase + '**/*.html',    included: false,
      watched:
      true
},
    { pattern: appBase + '**/*.css',    included: false,
      watched: true
},
    // Paths for debugging with    source maps in dev
       tools
    { pattern: appBase + '**/*.ts',    included: false,
      watched: false
},
    { pattern: appBase + '**/*.js.map',    included:
      false, watched:
      false
},
    { pattern: testingSrcBase +    '**/*.ts', included:
```

```
         false,
         watched: false },
      { pattern: testingBase + '**/*.js.map',    included:
         false,
         watched: false}
   ],
   // Proxied base paths for    loading assets
      proxies:
{
      // required for modules    fetched by SystemJS
      '/base/src/node_modules/': '/base/node_modules/'
},
   exclude: [],
   preprocessors: {},
   reporters: ['progress', 'kjhtml'],
   port: 9876,
   colors: true,
   logLevel: config.LOG_INFO,
   autoWatch: true,
   browsers: ['Chrome'],
   singleRun: false
})
}
```

The command, `karma start`, takes the karma config file path as argument and will start the karma test runner. The `npm run build` command is configured in `pretest` so that it will be executed before a test is run. It executes the `tsc -p src` command, a TypeScript compiler that transpiles the code in the `src` folder. The following screenshot illustrates the command window that executes these commands as per the configuration in `package.json` under the `scripts` item:

```
C:\Users\rajesh.g\Packt\Chapter8\mytodos>npm
  test
> my-todo@1.0.0 pretest
C:\Users\rajesh.g\Packt\Chapter8\mytodos
> npm run build
> my-todo@1.0.0 build
C:\Users\rajesh.g\Packt\Chapter8\mytodos
> tsc -p src/
> my-todo@1.0.0 test
C:\Users\rajesh.g\Packt\Chapter8\mytodos
> concurrently "npm run    build:watch" "karma
  start
  karma.conf.js"
```

Karma launches the application in a browser and runs all the tests in the specs. The `http-server` command will start the development server to host the `mytodo` Angular application. The result of the test execution is as shown:

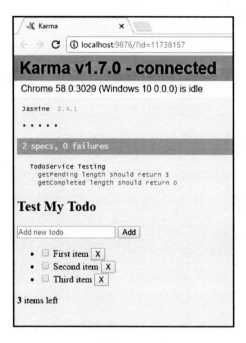

The test results of TodoService

Testing Angular components

We have just seen how to test a service in Angular application. Now, let's discuss testing an Angular component. Perform the following steps to create `AppComponent` for the application:

1. Create a file named `app.component.ts`.

2. Import modules such as `Component`, `TodoService`, and `Todo` that are necessary for the `AppComponent`, as shown:

   ```
   import { Component } from '@angular/core';
   import { Todo } from './todo';
   import { TodoService } from './todo.service';
   ```

3. Define the `AppComponent` class, as demonstrated:

```
export class AppComponent {}
```

4. Decorate the `AppComponent` class by the `@Component` attribute with the `selector`, `providers` and `templateUrl` metadata:

```
@Component({
    selector: 'my-app',
    templateUrl: './app.component.html',
    providers: [TodoService]
})
export class AppComponent {
}
```

5. Declare the `todos`, `todoService`, `newTodoText`, and `title` variables:

```
todos: Array<Todo>;
todoService: TodoService;
newTodoText = '';
title = 'Test My Todo App';
```

6. Define the constructor with `todoService` injected, as follows. Note that the constructor updates the `todos` with the `todos` returned from `todoService`:

```
constructor(todoService: TodoService)
{
        this.todoService = todoService;
        this.todos = todoService.todos;
}
```

7. Introduce the `addTodo()` function that calls the `add()` method of `TodoService` by passing the description of new `todo`, as illustrated:

```
addTodo()
{
        if (this.newTodoText.trim().length)
        {
            this.todoService.add(this.newTodoText);
            this.newTodoText = '';
        }
}
```

8. Introduce the `remove()` function that calls the `remove()` method of `TodoService` by passing a `todo` object to remove, as shown:

```
remove(todo: Todo)
{
        this.todoService.remove(todo);
}
```

9. Introduce the `removeCompleted()` function that calls the `removeCompleted()` method of `TodoService` to remove all the completed todo items:

```
removeCompleted()
{
        this.todoService.removeCompleted();
}
```

10. Introduce the `toggleCompletion()` function that calls the `toggleCompletion()` method of `TodoService` that toggles the value of the completed status of a `todo` item:

```
toggleCompletion(todo: Todo)
{
        todo.completed = !todo.completed;
}
```

The complete code snippet of `AppComponent` is this:

```
import { Component } from '@angular/core';
import { Todo } from './todo';
import { TodoService } from './todo.service';
@Component({
    selector: 'my-app',
    templateUrl: './app.component.html',
    providers: [TodoService]
})
export class AppComponent {
    todos: Array<Todo>;
    todoService: TodoService;
    newTodoText = '';
    title = 'Test My Todo App';
    constructor(todoService: TodoService) {
        this.todoService = todoService;
        this.todos = todoService.todos;
    }
    removeCompleted() {
        this.todoService.removeCompleted();
    }
```

```
    toggleCompletion(todo: Todo) {
        this.todoService.toggleCompletion(todo);
    }
    remove(todo: Todo) {
        this.todoService.remove(todo);
    }
    addTodo() {
        if (this.newTodoText.trim().length) {
            this.todoService.add(this.newTodoText);
            this.newTodoText = '';
        }
    }
}
```

We have the `AppComponent` in place now. The template for this `AppComponent` is defined in a template file, `app.component.html`.

Writing Specs for AppComponent

Let's write specs using Jasmine to test `AppComponent`:

1. Create a `app.component.spec.ts` file to write specs or tests for `AppComponent`.

2. Import modules such as `async`, `ComponentFixture`, `TestBed`, `FormsModule`, `By`, `DebugElement`, and `AppComponent` from Angular core.

3. Write the following `describe` global function and declare the necessary variables:

```
describe('AppComponent (templateUrl)', () => {
  let comp:    AppComponent;
  let fixture: ComponentFixture<AppComponent>;
  let de:      DebugElement;
  let el:      HTMLElement;
});
```

4. Then, create two `beforeEach` functions: one to compile the template and CSS, and the other to get the instance of the component. The code snippet is given here:

```
// async beforeEach
beforeEach(async(() => {
    TestBed.configureTestingModule({
        imports: [FormsModule],
        declarations: [ AppComponent ], // declare the
test component
    })
    .compileComponents();  // compile template and css
}));
// synchronous beforeEach
beforeEach(() => {
    fixture = TestBed.createComponent(AppComponent);
    comp = fixture.componentInstance; // AppComponent
test instance
    // query for the title <h1> by CSS element
        selector
    de = fixture.debugElement.query(By.css('h1'));
    el = de.nativeElement;
});
```

For each test, we may end up repeating the same code to initialize or to clear some objects. To ease the work of the developer, Jasmine provides the `beforeEach` and `afterEach` global functionalities that run before and after executing each test method respectively.

5. Finally, add the `it` test or specs functions to verify the expectations, as shown:

```
it('no title in the DOM until manually call
`detectChanges`', () => {
expect(el.textContent).toEqual('');
});
it('should display original title', () => {
    fixture.detectChanges();
    expect(el.textContent).toContain(comp.title);
});
it('should display a different test title', () => {
    comp.title = 'Test My Todo';
    fixture.detectChanges();
    expect(el.textContent).toContain('Test My Todo');
});
```

The complete code snippet of `app.component.spec.ts` is as follows:

```
import { async, ComponentFixture, TestBed } from '@angular/core/testing';
import { FormsModule } from '@angular/forms';
import { By }              from '@angular/platform-browser';
import { DebugElement }    from '@angular/core';
import { AppComponent } from './app.component';
describe('AppComponent (templateUrl)', () => {
  let comp:     AppComponent;
  let fixture: ComponentFixture<AppComponent>;
  let de:       DebugElement;
  let el:       HTMLElement;
  // async beforeEach
  beforeEach(async(() => {
    TestBed.configureTestingModule({
      imports: [FormsModule],
      declarations: [ AppComponent ], // declare the test component
    })
    .compileComponents();  // compile template and css
  }));
  // synchronous beforeEach
  beforeEach(() => {
    fixture = TestBed.createComponent(AppComponent);
    comp = fixture.componentInstance; // AppComponent test instance
    // query for the title <h1> by CSS element selector
    de = fixture.debugElement.query(By.css('h1'));
    el = de.nativeElement;
  });
  it('no title in the DOM until manually call `detectChanges`', () => {
    expect(el.textContent).toEqual('');
  });
  it('should display original title', () => {
    fixture.detectChanges();
    expect(el.textContent).toContain(comp.title);
  });
  it('should display a different test title', () => {
    comp.title = 'Test My Todo';
    fixture.detectChanges();
    expect(el.textContent).toContain('Test My Todo');
  });
});
```

Running the specs or tests of AppComponent

Execute the `npm test` command in the command-line window, and the application will start and the tests will be run for you. The following screenshot shows the result of tests or specs that ran against `AppComponent`:

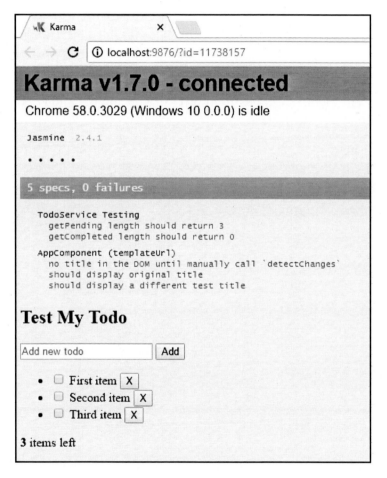

Test result of AppComponent

Unit testing a mock service

Keeping the components lean by injecting the services into it enables us to write unit tests with a mock service. We can mock the injected service by mimicking the service behavior using its interface:

```
class MockTodoService extends TodoService    {
    getPending() {
        return [];
    }
}
```

Here, we created a mock of an existing todo service by extending and overriding the getPending method to return an empty array.

We can test this using testBed, instructing how to use the mock service, MockTodoService instead of the actual service, TodoService, as follows:

```
beforeEach(async(() => {
    TestBed.configureTestingModule({
      providers: [
      {
          provide: TodoService,
          useClass:   MockTodoService
      }
    ]})
    .compileComponents();
}));
```

Here, we instructed how to use MockTodoService instead of TodoService, and we can sky the outcome of testing, as follows:

```
it('should return empty array   when getPending method is fired', () => {
    let service =   fixture.debugElement.injector.get(TodoService);
    spyOn(service, 'getPending').and.returnValue([]);
});
```

Here, it gets the mock service, MockTodoService, from fixture and adds a spyOn override to pretend that there are no pending todo items in the list.

Summary

Hurray! We learned the basics of writing automated testing for Angular applications.

We started this chapter with an introduction to the Jasmine framework and learned how to write effective tests and run them automatically. Then, we learned how to test components and services using the Jasmine framework and assert the behavior of the application. Finally, we discussed mocking a service and testing it using spyOn.

In the next chapter, we will discuss some of the new topics in Angular and .NET Core.

9
What's New in Angular and ASP.NET Core

We started this book with a discussion on Angular, building a hello world application, and the core architecture of Angular. Then, we dived into the building blocks of Angular. Next, we discussed the basics of TypeScript and how to use TypeScript in writing Angular applications. Later, we walked through creating an Angular single-page application in Visual Studio and learned about RESTful services and creating a RESTful service using Web API for Angular applications. After that, we did a complete step-by-step walk-through on creating an application using Angular, ASP.NET MVC, and Web API in Visual Studio. Finally, we learned about testing Angular applications using Karma and Jasmine.

This chapter will discuss what is new in Angular and ASP.NET Core. We will cover the following topics:

- Ahead-of-Time compilation
- Update on Templates
- Introducing titlecase pipes
- Simplified parameter passing in HTTP
- Overriding templates in testing
- Introducing the Meta service
- New form validators
- Introducing ParamMap in a router
- Introducing .NET Core 1.0
- Cross-platform development with the .NET Execution Environment

What's new in Angular

The Angular team has dropped Angular 3 and proceeded with Angular 4 as they have decided to follow semantic versioning. This helps standardize the version for major, minor, and patch releases. The semantic version will have three segments in the version numbering. Any breaking change in syntax or concept will be considered as major and the first segment version number will be incremented. Any new features added will be considered as minor and the second segment version number will be incremented, and for any bug fixes, the third segment version number will be incremented, considering them as patch:

Fig 01: Semantic versioning

Ahead-of-Time compilation

Angular introduces a major change that generates JavaScript code when building your application. This enables you to know whether there are any errors in templates when building rather than being notified at runtime. Also, it enables the application to run faster as the code generation has already been completed during the build phase. The new Angular view engine generates less code when using **Ahead-of-Time (AoT)**.

Update on templates

As the template is a real HTML tag for the web component, Angular introduced a new `ng-template` tag for templates. Angular enabled us to use `else` in `ngIf` in templates, as follows:

```
<div *ngIf="isOld; then  content else new_content">placeholder</div>
<ng-template  #content><h2>old content body.</h2></ng-template>
<ng-template  #new_content><h2>body of new content.</h2></ng-template>
```

Here, if `isOld` is true, the content of the old template will be displayed. Otherwise, the content of the new template will be displayed.

Next, let's discuss the as keyword added to the template syntax. It is introduced to simplify the syntax of let. It enables us to store the results in a template variable:

```
<ul>
    <li *ngFor="let book of   books | slice:0:10 as topTenBooks; index as
idx">
        {{ topTenBooks.length - idx   }}: { book.name }}
    </li>
</ul>
```

Here, we used the as keyword to store the result of slice in the topTenBooks variable and further referenced it in the li tag. Note that we also gave an alias name, i, to index, which is the short form of the let i = index syntax.

We can also use the as keyword and async together, as shown:

```
<ul>
    <li *ngFor="let book of   books$ | async">
        {{ book.name }}
    </li>
</ul>
<h3>{{ ( books$ |   async)?.length }} books</h3>
```

Here, we have made our books collection as Observable. So, we have iterated through the array of books returned from Observable. Note that we also display the number of books returned from the Observable. However, this leads to a performance overhead as the async pipe used will rerun if there are changes. Further improvement, as follows, avoids such performance overhead:

```
<div *ngIf="books$ | async as   books">
    <ul>
        <li *ngFor="let book of   books">
            {{ book.name }}
        </li>
    </ul>
<div>
<h3>{{  books.length }}   books</h3>
```

Here, we used the as keyword to store a piped value in a parent component. Note that we used async only once.

Introducing titlecase pipes

A titlecase pipe changes the first letter of a word to uppercase. We can use titlecase as follows:

```
<p>{{ 'rajesh gunasundaram'   | titlecase }}</p>
 the parsed HTML will be    <p>Rajesh Gunasundaram</p>
```

Simplified parameter passing in HTTP

Angular has simplified passing parameters to HTTP requests. In the next code snippet, note that we pass a value to `sort` parameter in the HTTP GET call:

```
http.get('http://www.programmerguide.net/api/articles`,   { params: { sort:
'ascending' } });
```

Overriding templates in testing

Sometimes it is necessary to override templates during testing. Angular has now simplified overriding templates, as follows:

```
TestBed.overrideTemplate(BookComponent,   '<h1>{{book.title}}</h1>');
```

Before that, we need to build JSON and pass it.

Introducing the Meta service

Angular has introduced a new service called the Meta service that simplifies updating or getting the `meta` tags:

```
@Component({
  selector: 'book-list',
  template: `<h1>Book   List</h1>`
})
export class BookComponent {
  constructor(meta: Meta) {
    meta.addTag({ name: 'author',   content: 'Rajesh Gunasundaram' });
  }
}
```

New form validators

New validator combines the existing validators such as `required`, `minLength`, `maxLength`, `email`, and `pattern`. Also, a new directive, `compareWith`, is introduced to compare options from a `select` control, as shown:

```
<select [compareWith]="byId"   [(ngModel)]="selectedBook">
    <option *ngFor="let book of   books"
[ngValue]="book">{{book.title}}</option>
</select>
byId(p1: BookModel, p2:   BookModel) {
    return p1.id === p2.id;
}
```

Introducing ParamMap in router

Angular has introduced a new interface, `ParamMap`, to map the parameters in a URL. We can use `paramMap` or `queryParamMap` to access parameters of a URL. `ParamMap` has methods such as `get()` to get a value or `getAll()` to get all the values of the query parameters, as follows:

```
const id =   this.route.snapshot.paramMap.get('bookId');
this.bookService.get(id).subscribe(b   => this.book = b);
```

In an observable, we need to use `ParamMap` as illustrated:

```
this.route.paramMap
  .map((params: ParamMap) =>   params.get('bookId'))
  .switchMap(id =>   this.bookService.get(id))
  .subscribe(b => this.book =   b);
```

Introducing .NET Core 1.0

In this section, we will cover the basics of .NET Core 1.0 as a platform and the components involved in it.

The .NET Core 1.0 platform was reinvented for various reasons. The web stack of ASP.NET was pretty old and was started back in .NET Framework 1.0. ASP.NET was overweighed with a lot of old and unused code. Even the code it not used as it becomes unavoidable from loading them. The biggest one is `System.Web`, which is a linkage between the old ASP.NET and today's ASP.NET. MVC and Web API are trying to isolate themselves from `System.Web`.

Self-hosting of ASP.NET, MVC, and Web API is one of the objectives so that they can be hosted independently of the server platform. However, it was tied to the Windows platform on IIS. This becomes an issue when an application needs to be retested for any new bugs that were introduced due to the newer version of .NET when updated to servers as these depend on machine-level versions of .NET, and it is not possible to isolate the version of .NET from your application so that it can run independently of the newer version of .NET.

The ASP.NET team had decided to rewrite the code from the ground up as the time frame was vulnerable by the amount of code that had to be loaded in, compiled, written to disk, loaded back into memory, and then executed. For good, a lot of things have been changed in .NET Core 1.0, and it is incredibly different from every other version of ASP.NET. That's why it is good to call it with a new name and new version as it is not an incremental change.

A key difference is that .NET Core 1.0 is cross-platform and open source. .NET Core 1.0 is a single platform that combines both the concepts of MVC and Web API into one solid set of APIs and all the legacy code is gone. Everything is a dependency in .NET Core 1.0. We can develop a .NET application as small as we want it to be. Some parts of .NET Core are now a NuGet. So, you can load only the required assemblies from NuGet, and this leads to a small memory footprint compared to the previous versions of ASP.NET.

Multiple deployment support is possible today in .NET Core 1.0, and this enables us to deploy to clouds, such as Azure, AWS, and other cloud services. You can host it in IIS, or it can be self-hosted, which enables us to execute from the command line. .NET Core 1.0 supports true cross-platform, and it can be hosted on both Windows and OSX or Linux:

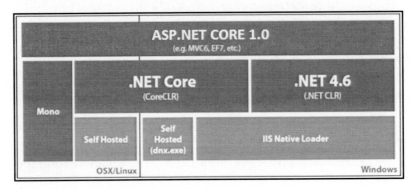

Fig 02: Building blocks of ASP.NET Core 1.0

As shown in the preceding figure, .NET Core includes a new CLR that is supported on both OSX/Linux and Windows. ASP.NET can also run on top of Mono. Using the native IIS loader, we can load and host our applications in IIS. This native IIS loader routes requests directly to ASP.NET without the need to go through ISAPI filters and others. On the Windows platform, you can also self-host the application from the command line using a tool called `dotnet.exe`. .NET Core 1.0 also supports self-hosting on Linux and OSX and can be done using some sort of tool, such as `dotnet.exe`, so that the application can be run just with a command line.

The self-hosted solutions are similar to Node. Running Node and then the root of your application is very similar to the way that self-hosting works in .NET Core with the `dotnet.exe` tool. So, being cross-platform supported, the code you write will not necessarily care about where it's being hosted.

.NET Core is the new cross-platform and a subset of the .NET Framework. The .NET Core is meant to be as small as possible. The CoreCLR or .NET Core Framework is a subset of the .NET Framework. So, all functionalities will not be available in .NET Core. For example, sending a mail is achieved by the mail subsystem inside the .NET Framework in the System.Net namespace. However, this functionality doesn't exist, and it can be accomplished using some open source solutions.

The .NET Core team wanted to compose everything via NuGet packages. So, everything preceding the CLR and C# and VB compilers is a NuGet package. The .NET Core 1.0 is really the bootstrap and the CLR is not a whole. The code knows how to load up an application and get it started, and then the CLR actually manages the execution of that code. Everything else will be a NuGet package. MVC looks at static files doing logging, configuration, and identity; they're all just packages that can be added to a project. So, as you talk about creating thicker or thinner applications, you can make decisions about what to include in your project. Everything in ASP.NET is optional.

The ASP.NET 5 team has tried to embrace the Node package manager for different sorts of tooling support, using npm or Bower for client-side library support, using Grunt and Gulp for build automation, and NuGet for .NET packages.

Cross-platform development with the .NET Execution Environment

In this section, we will discuss what the roles of the full .NET Framework, the Core CLR, and the DNX are. We will start by explaining how the .NET Framework developers have used the Execution Environment since the beginning of .NET. Also, we will see Mono and .NET Core. Then, we will see some guidelines to decide which framework to use. Finally, we will see how the DNX binds everything together.

The traditional .NET Framework

Since the beginnings of .NET, the desktop and console applications have been bootstrapped by executable files and the traditional ASP.NET applications are bootstrapped by IIS using an ISAPI DLL. The applications written in any language supported by .NET are compiled to an assembly. An assembly is an EXE or DLL file containing **Intermediate Language (IL)**. This IL file needs to be compiled to native code as the operating systems and CPUs don't understand IL, and this is called **just-in-time (JIT)** compiling.

JIT compiles the IL code to native code just before it executes on the machine where the assemblies are deployed. The JIT functionality is part of the .NET CLR or common language runtime.

The CLR is responsible for loading assemblies, checking types, and garbage collection. So, it is necessary to install the .NET Framework on the machine application runs. The big stack of classes and other types are available. It contains all types needed for Windows Forms, WCF, WPF, web forms, and types usable across these frameworks, such as file handling, reading, and manipulating XML, drawing, and cryptography. All applications use some of these classes.

The CLR is specifically designed to run on Windows. Also, some of the classes in the FCL are specifically for Windows. `System.web` is an assembly containing classes that are tied to IIS and therefore Windows. building blocks of legacy .NET Framework are as follows:

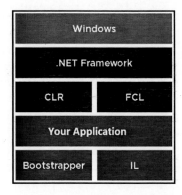

Fig 03: Building blocks of legacy .NET Framework

Mono Cross-platform .NET Framework

Mono is an open source version of the .NET Framework developed by the community. It uses the exact same principles that Microsoft .NET Framework uses. It's compatible with the Microsoft .NET Framework. Even if you don't use ASP.NET 5, you can create assemblies on a Windows machine using the Microsoft .NET Framework and Visual Studio and run them on Mono on a Linux machine. So, an important difference with Microsoft .NET Framework is that it is cross-platform. Versions are available for Windows, macOS, and Linux. It's also used as the basis for Xamarin, which runs .NET on Android and iOS.

NuGet package manager

Microsoft has introduced NuGet to manage packages and download them easily for development. NuGet is a central place to get the libraries. Developers of these libraries and frameworks can easily apply new versions or bug fixes to NuGet. Microsoft began to use NuGet for assemblies that would normally be in the FCL. MVC is installed as a NuGet package in the application and not machine-wide like the FCL. This enables different applications to use different versions of MVC without the need to install different versions of the .NET Framework. Distributing MVC via NuGet gave Microsoft the ability to update MVC "out of band" with the .NET Framework, which enabled MVC to evolve much faster with more frequent updates. This was the upbeat of a completely modular framework class library with .NET Core.

CoreFx and CoreCLR in .NET Core

Through the years, .NET has been reinvented multiple times. There is a .NET Framework for Windows Desktop, Windows Store apps, and Windows Phone. We also have the framework we used all along for ASP.NET 4 and earlier apps. Microsoft invented a way to share code between all the different platforms with portable class libraries and with the concept of universal apps. However, wouldn't it be a lot easier if we had a version of .NET for all platforms? Not only for Microsoft that has to keep all these stacks up to date, but also for us developers who have to learn and maintain all these versions. The purpose of .NET Core is to be the one .NET version that rules them all, and it all starts with ASP.NET! Another motivation for .NET Core is the need to reduce the overall footprint. From an ASP.NET perspective, using system.web isn't really an option anymore. Also, having a huge .NET Framework on a machine that causes versioning problems and contains lots of stuff you don't need is cumbersome. In this cloud-driven world, being fixed to Windows isn't of this time anymore. The most exciting feature of .NET Core is that it can run across operating systems using a new DNX.

Just like the full .NET Framework, .NET Core also consists of two parts: a common language runtime, which is now portable and goes by the name CoreCLR, and a class library called CoreFX. CoreFX contains a set of types common across every .NET application. It doesn't include complete frameworks such as WPF or web forms like the FCL in the full .NET Framework. There are, for example, classes to manipulate files and classes that are collections like a list. The different assemblies of CoreFX are individually distributed via NuGet. You have to get everything else you need outside of CoreFX, such as the MVC framework, from NuGet. Not only is CoreFX distributed in a NuGet package, the CoreCLR is as well. The .NET Core is what Microsoft calls cloud optimized. That basically means that it's lightweight. It is not only much smaller than the full .NET Framework, it also contains optimizations:

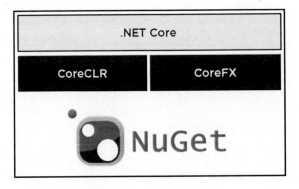

Fig 04: Building blocks of .NET Core

Just like any NuGet package, .NET Core can be restored from NuGet per project. When you publish your app to a server, you can also publish the CoreCLR with your app. So, there is no machine-wide installation necessary anymore. Each app on the server can have its own .NET Core version without affecting other applications. It's also great that the .NET Core as well as the DNX are open source software. This means that besides Microsoft, the community is working on it, and you can also work on it. It also ensures that the projects will be continued should Microsoft decide to cease working on them:

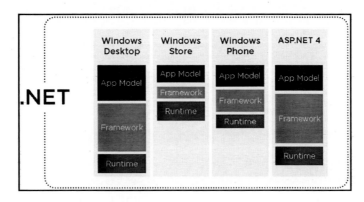

Fig 05: .NET applications framework

Choosing a Framework

How do you make a choice on which framework to use? Where the right version of the .NET Framework or Mono has to be installed machine-wide to support your app, you can have applications using different versions of .NET Core on one server. You can also update one application to use a newer version of .NET Core without affecting the others. With the .NET Framework or Mono, you have the best chance to use the existing code. It offers a huge selection of classes and other types. CoreFX is a different class library, and you will probably have to refactor when using the existing code. Also, CoreFX has a much smaller choice of usable types, and not everything you're used to is available using extra packages. It is an ecosystem that still has to evolve where the FCL is very complete, and it is proven technology. However, it contains a lot you probably don't need. Using Mono or .NET Core are your choices if your app has to run cross-platform. The .NET Framework runs on Windows only. Targeting multiple frameworks makes sense if you're developing component libraries for use in your own business or if you want to distribute them commercially. Your libraries can be used by applications using all the chosen frameworks.

Alternatively, maybe you have to write an app now and decide the framework it has to run on later. In the next section, we'll see the role that DNX plays in all this:

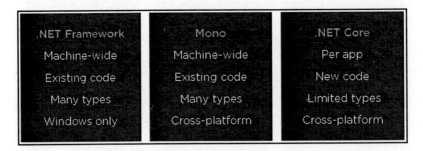

Fig 06: Criteria of Choosing the Frameworks

The Dotnet Execution Environment- DNX

The primary role of DNX is to run the .NET applications by hosting the CLR in the framework. The newly introduced command-line interface dotnet cli has the executable part of the DNX. Dotnet cli helps run applications and restore packages that are specified in the `project.json`.

The DNX command-line application has its own process to execute an application instead of Windows or IIS executing the app; the DNX hosts the CLR instead of the operating system. The DNX will look for an entry point in the form of a `Main` method and run the application from there. As a separate process runs the app and thus there is no dependency on the operating system anymore, the DNX command-line application can be developed for multiple operating systems, such as Windows, Linux, and macOS. Now, the app you developed in Visual Studio can run cross-platform. There is a DNX version available for each .NET Framework per operating system. There can also be versions supporting different CPU architectures. For the full .NET Framework, for example, there is an x86 version and an x64 version.

Different versions of the DNX can coexist on one machine. You can either install them in a central location for the whole machine, or you can choose to make the DNX part of the deployment of your application. No machine-wide installation is needed at all using that method. If you publish the app in Visual Studio, you have to choose for what version of the DNX configured in the framework section of the `project.json` you want to publish. That version of the DNX will then be distributed with the deployed app:

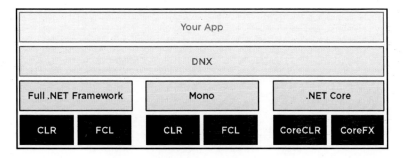

Fig 07: Building blocks of DNX

The DNX is part of dotnet cli that exposes its functionality in the dotnet command-line application. When you run a DNX app in Visual Studio, all Visual Studio does is to execute a command line. When you run, for example, it will execute `dotnet run`, which will put the DNX to work. While running the app, the DNX also supports debugging. When you add NuGet packages to the `project.json` file, it will just execute `dotnet restore`. Also, there are commands for compiling and publishing the app among others. Dotnet cli is just a command given on the command line, so it doesn't need Visual Studio to execute. You can execute it directly by just typing in the commands or use some other tool to invoke it. An example of such a tool is Visual Studio Code, which also runs cross-platform. The `dotnet` command will be used in ASP.NET 5 versions RC2 and higher. The different command-line applications, such as DNX and DNU, are united in the dotnet command-line. When you execute dotnet restore, for example, it will read the `project.json` file and download and install packages where needed. So, the DNX is not only a runtime environment, it is also an SDK. The runtime part kicks in when you execute `dotnet run` in an app's folder.

Deployment options

There are four options for deployment. All the options are supported by the dotnet command-line interface. You can choose to copy over the app's project, let the DNX restore the packages, and run the app. A compatible DNX version has to be preinstalled; use the CLI command dotnet run for this one.

You can also let the CLI compile the project on your development machine. Copy over the assemblies and run:

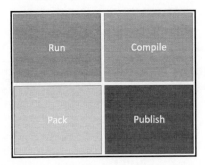

Fig 08: Deployment Options

There is also the option to natively compile an app using a command-line switch. This means that instead of assemblies with IL, native binaries that can be directly executed without the help of the DNX or any .NET Framework are generated.

There is also an option to package your application into a NuGet package to easily share your project using dotnet pack. The package will contain support for all the configured frameworks in the `project.json` file. You can then upload it to a NuGet feed either globally or for your company only.

The final option is to let dotnet cli publish the app for you using dotnet publish.

All the required assemblies and the DNX itself is included in the deployment. As the deployed DNX is OS-specific, this option won't work without extra effort if you're deploying across operating systems.

Publishing with Visual Studio

We will learn to deploy an application using Visual Studio. If we right-click on the web node of our project, we can pick Publish, and Publish will allow us to pick a target. Visual Studio will ask you to provide the name of the publishing profile to create and store the publishing profile for future use:

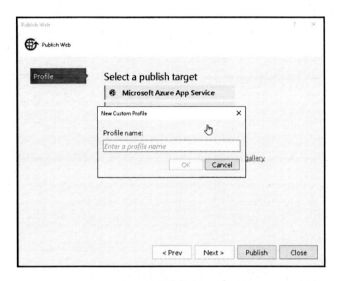

Fig 09: Creating a publishing profile

We can choose Azure Web Apps, filesystem, and other mode of deployment. In **Settings**, we can also pick which configuration we will use and which of the DNX versions to use. Here, you will only see options that match what you specified in the `project.json` file under the frameworks section. Finally, we can Publish the application:

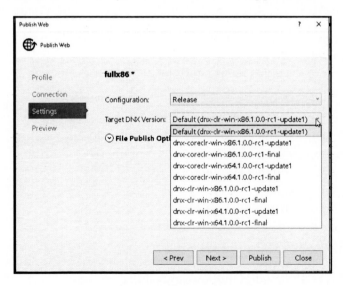

Fig 10: Choosing DNX version

When published, it first runs the `prepare` statement and then the `prepublish` in order to package it all up in the temporary folder, and then it literally copies it out to the filesystem. Once the publishing is successful, open the command-line interface and navigate to the publish folder.

Note that the folder includes the commands and shell scripts that are defined in the project file. Also, note that the `approot` folder contains the packages and the runtimes necessary for the application.

If you are on the Windows platform, we can use the web command to start the application. You can simply open a browser and navigate to `localhost` with the `5000` port, and we can see our application actually running. The application is running directly from the command shell and not under IIS.

Publishing with dotnet command-line interface

Let's see how we can publish using dotnet command-line interface. From Visual Studio, open up a command shell directly in the project folder of our application. If we look at the `DOTNET` command, we can see that it has a number of commands where you can build your projects and install dependencies, especially NuGet-based dependencies. You can handle packages and publish the application. The following is the command that shows the Windows result that shows various options and arguments in the command:

```
C:\Rajesh\Packt\Angular2>dotnet
.NET Command Line Interface
Usage: dotnet [common-options] [command] [arguments]
```

- Arguments:
  [command]: The command to execute
  [arguments]: Arguments to pass to the command
- Common Options: (passed before the command):
  `-v|--verbose` Enable verbose output
- Common Commands:
  `new`: Initialize a basic .NET project
  `restore`: Restore dependencies specified in the .NET project
  `compile`: Compiles a .NET project
  `publish`: Publishes a .NET project for deployment (including the `runtime`) `run`: Compiles and immediately executes a .NET project
  `repl`: Launch an interactive session (read, eval, print, loop)
  `pack`: Creates a NuGet package

The dotnet command-line interface is useful in that you can actually script all these processes, you can have it install the dependencies, run the build, and then publish it. So, it provides an easy way to automate a lot of these tasks. In fact, Visual Studio is just automating this using the Dotnet tool.

The published folder contains the code of the application, all the dependencies, both the client dependencies, the tooling dependencies, and the NuGet dependencies, and contains the entire version of the runtime that's required. We can take this folder and put on any box and run. If you want to package this up for Linux or OS 10, you'll need a version of the runtime that is appropriate for those platforms, like CoreCLR would be. This folder has the self-contained application and can run on any browser. This doesn't use any framework that's installed on the machine; it's all within that one folder, completely portable.

Deploying to IIS

We need to ensure that the `HttpPlatformHandler` module that acts as a reverse proxy is installed when you deploy to an IIS server. When the request comes in, IIS forwards it to another process, which is typically a command-line application. IIS will start and stop the process when needed and take care of concurrency.

In the IIS management application, our application is considered as another website, and can be configured in IIS. We need to inform IIS to execute the DNX when our application gets a request. We can achieve it using the `web.config` present in the project's folder. IIS still uses `web.config` for `HttpPlatformHandler`:

```xml
<?xml version="1.0" encoding="utf-8"?>
<configuration>
  <system.webServer>
    <handlers>
      <add name="httpPlatformHandler" path="*" verb="*"
           modules="httpPlatformHandler" resourceType="Unspecified"/>
    </handlers>
    <httpPlatform processPath="%DNX_PATH%" arguments="%DNX_ARGS%"
                  stdoutLogEnabled="false" startupTimeLimit="3600"/>
  </system.webServer>
</configuration>
```

Fig 11: Configuring HttpPlatformHandler in the web.config file

The `HttpPlatformHandler` extension is registered with IIS and is instructed to execute the batch file starting the DNX process when it gets a request. So, let's configure the app in IIS.

To configure our application, start the IIS manager. Right-click on the root server node and choose **Add Website**, type the application name, and an application pool will automatically be generated for our application:

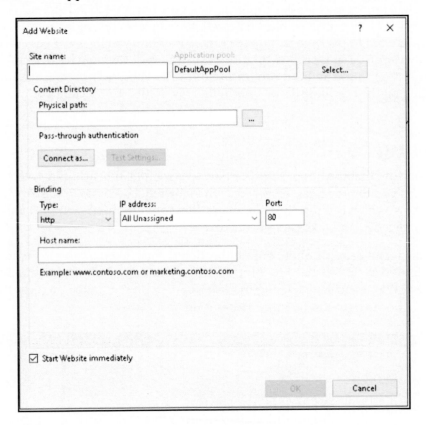

Fig 12: Adding a website to IIS

Set the path to the wwwroot folder of the published application in the physical path textbox and click on **OK**. As the CLR is running in the exclusive process, we need to set **No Managed Code** under **.NET CLR version** on the application pool:

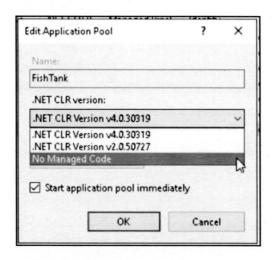

Fig 13: Setting No Managed Code in .NET CLR for App Pool

We are doing this because we don't need IIS to host the CLR for our application. Clicking on **OK** and browsing to the localhost port 8080 will launch our application. In this way, we can use the features of IIS to power DNX application similar to any other web application hosted in IIS.

Deploying to Microsoft Azure

Azure deployment using its app service is very smooth. When an application is published to Azure, a new virtual machine is created, or it is hosted on an existing virtual machine that runs IIS, with HttpPlatformHandler installed. The deployment process is the same as deploying to IIS on a local server.

A new website has to be created in IIS and the published content has to be uploaded to the server. All this can be done by creating a publish profile in Visual Studio, choosing **Microsoft Azure App Service**. We may need to log in to an Azure account, choose a subscription, and create a new app in Azure by giving a name. The URL will be `yourappname.azurewebsites.net`. Under **Settings**, we need to choose the DNX and click on **Publish**. Browsing to `yourappname.azurewebsites.net` will bring your application running from Azure:

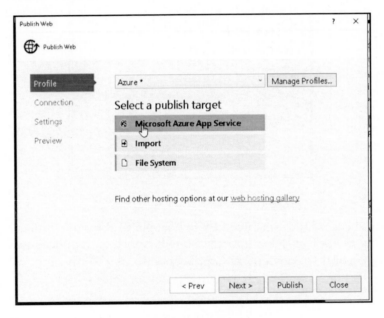

Fig 14: Selecting publish target

Deploying to Linux and macOS

Let's look at deploying apps from Visual Studio to Linux or macOS. We can also develop the application in the Linux or macOS platform using Visual Studio Code.

First, install a DNX for the framework, .NET Core or Mono. Next, copy the whole Visual Studio project, including source code and `project.json` and no assemblies.

Then, use the dotnet cli to restore all the NuGet packages. This will include the assemblies the DNX needs to host the CLR in .NET Core. However, NuGet packages can have dependencies on other packages, so there has to be some kind of list of all packages needed before a restore can occur. The compilation of such a list takes time because all packages have to be inspected to see what their dependencies are. The lock file contains this compiled list, so the figuring out has to be done only once. All the subsequent restores use the lock file, provided that the list of packages in `project.json` hasn't changed.

Finally, instruct the DNX to run the program using Kestrel as the web server. The DNX will use Kestrel as an entry point, and Kestrel will then host the app. Kestrel gives me a notification that the app is running on port 5000. Browsing to `localhost` as the domain name with port 5000 launches our application in Linux or macOS.

Summary

That's all, folks! We discussed what's new in Angular and .NET Core 1.0. We started with the new features introduced in Angular. We explored the improvements done on the various existing approaches in Angular. Finally, we looked at .NET Core 1.0 and the cross-platform development with the .NET Execution Environment in detail. We learned the difference between the full .NET Framework, .NET Core, and Mono. Also, we covered what DNX is and its role in developing .NET apps in a completely new way.

Index

CONTENTS

Unit 1 IN MY OWN WORDS ... AND IN SOMEONE ELSE'S TOO: reading and comparing the written lives of fictional characters and real people; identifying the features of biography and autobiography.

Chewing the Cud

In late 1995, my wife, Myrle, and I walked into a London cinema to see a film called *Babe*. We had no idea what to expect.

Eight years or more had gone by since I had sold the world rights of a book of mine, *The Sheep-Pig*, to an Australian company, and I knew nothing at all about their adaptation of Book into Film.

We took our seats. The opening credits came up on the huge screen. Among them:

ADAPTED FROM THE BOOK
BY **DICK KING-SMITH**

We nudged each other.

Myrle and I sat enthralled throughout the film. It was soon plain to us that the adaptation from the book had been wonderfully well done.

There were differences, of course – there always are when you change something from one medium to another. There were additional pieces of action, and quite an array of new characters – another dog, the cat, that marvellous duck – but the director had stuck pretty faithfully to the central theme of my original story: the tale of an orphaned piglet who is adopted by a farmer and by his sheep-dog. This little pig, by virtue of his intelligence and determination, his courage, and especially through his realization that politeness pays, comes eventually to win the Grand Challenge Sheep-dog Trials. One particular thing about the film that delighted me was that, as soon as I set eyes on the actor who played Farmer Hoggett, I saw to my amazement that he was the spitting image of the imaginary figure I'd had in my head when I wrote the book all those years before.

I've seen *Babe* six times now and every time I've laughed and I've cried, but of course at that first viewing we had no idea that the film would becomes such a huge international success. During the many years that it was in the making, I'd written masses of other children's books. But *The Sheep-Pig* was to be the one that would bring me so much publicity and do me such a lot of good.

If you were to ask me to choose a favourite from among the dozens and dozens of books I've produced, I would probably say I think it may be the best.

It's always nice for me to think that, in a funny way, *Babe* was born here, in the little village where we live. I mean that he was born in my head, in my imagination, thanks to our annual village Summer Fête.

One particular year I was in charge of the Guess-the-Weight-of-the-Pig stall, and I must, I suppose, have thought as I stood upon the village green, recording people's guesses and taking their money, that it was a shame that such a lovely little pink pig should end up, once he was big enough, in the deep-freeze.

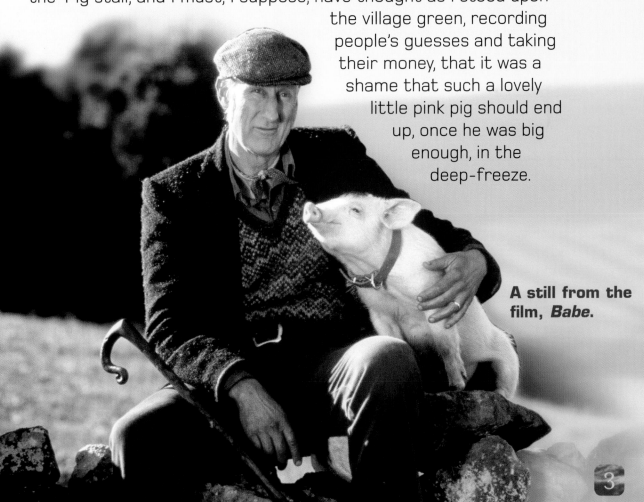

A still from the film, *Babe*.

3

Suppose fate had something quite different in store for him? Suppose he should go and live on a farm, with a sheep-dog as his foster-mother? Suppose he should want to do what she did?

He couldn't be a sheep-dog.

But he could be a sheep-pig.

For twenty years and more I have come to think of myself as a writer. But for all the early part of my life I thought of myself as a farmer, and, indeed, between 1947 and 1967, I was one.

Often, in my dreams, we are still at our first farm, Woodlands Farm. The children are still small (though in fact one of them now has a grandchild about the same age).

Occasionally in these dreams, I drive a tractor or work in a remembered field, but I am more likely to be in the farm buildings, preparing food in the old disused pigsty, feeding the pigs in the barn or the calves in the stables or the hens in the loft or the rabbits in a loose-box. Woodlands Farm was like that – everything lived in an unexpected place. Mostly, of course, I'm in the cowshed, doing the milking, always somehow seeming to be behindhand, I'm late, I'll never be finished in time for the milk lorry, get a move on, do.

For Myrle and me, that first farm was a bit like the toy farms that each of us had played with as small children. It was stocked with practically every sort of animal you could think of. It was a bit of a muddle, but a cosy muddle. It was full of interest, then in reality, now in dreams.

Dick King–Smith

Charles Dickens

Charles and Fanny Dickens went to two small schools in Chatham. The fearsome old lady who ran the first school they attended, used to rap Charles's head with her knuckles to make him pay attention! However their second teacher recognized both children's talents.

One day, while Charles was out walking with his father, they came within sight of a beautiful ivy-clad house, with great bow windows, a white-columned doorway, and spacious gardens. This was Gad's Hill Place. Some day, his father told him, if he worked hard, he might live in a house like that – perhaps the very same one. Charles was never to forget it.

Meanwhile his father's free-spending habits had begun to cause serious concern. Late in 1822, John Dickens' employers transferred him to London. After finishing the school term, Charles joined his family.

Poverty was tightening its grip on the growing family: after a year they had nothing left to pawn. Though Fanny went to the Royal Academy of Music, Charles's own education seemed finished. As he turned twelve, in 1824, he was sent to work.

For 12 hours a day he laboured in Warren's blacking warehouse down by the river. It was a filthy, half-rotten, rat-infested place, and the work was sheer drudgery: tying paper round pots of blacking paste, then gluing on the labels. His high hopes plunged.

Worse still, his father had been arrested – and his mother and the four younger children had gone to live with him in Marshalsea debtors' prison. Charles and Fanny visited them at weekends. Meanwhile, Charles lived alone in cheap lodgings, eking out his pennies day by day.

His miserable situation lasted only a few months, but the impression it left on him was life-long. The ordeals of many outcast children in his books showed how deeply he was scarred.

From *Great Lives: Charles Dickens* by Nigel Hunter

Boy

I was homesick during the whole of my first term at St Peter's. Homesickness is a bit like seasickness. You don't know how awful it is till you get it, and when you do, it hits you right in the top of the stomach and you want to die. The only comfort is that both homesickness and seasickness are instantly curable. The first goes away the moment you walk out of the school grounds and the second is forgotten as soon as the ship enters port.

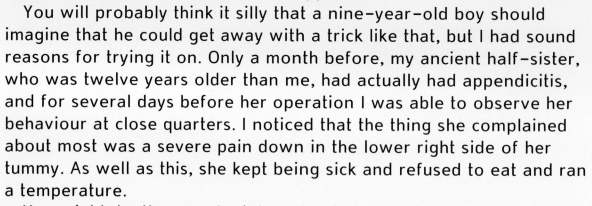

I was so devastatingly homesick during my first two weeks that I set about devising a stunt for getting myself sent back home, even if it was only for a few days. My idea was that I should all of a sudden develop an attack of acute appendicitis.

You will probably think it silly that a nine-year-old boy should imagine that he could get away with a trick like that, but I had sound reasons for trying it on. Only a month before, my ancient half-sister, who was twelve years older than me, had actually had appendicitis, and for several days before her operation I was able to observe her behaviour at close quarters. I noticed that the thing she complained about most was a severe pain down in the lower right side of her tummy. As well as this, she kept being sick and refused to eat and ran a temperature.

You might, by the way, be interested to know that this sister had her appendix removed not in a fine hospital operating-room full of bright lights and gowned nurses but on our own nursery table at home by the local doctor and his anaesthetist. In those days it was fairly common practice for a doctor to arrive at your own house with a bag of instruments, then drape a sterile sheet over the most convenient table and get on with it. On this occasion I can remember lurking in the corridor outside the nursery while the operation was going on. My other sisters were with me, and we stood there spellbound, listening to the soft medical murmurs coming from behind the locked door and picturing the patient with her stomach sliced open like a lump of beef.

We could even smell the sickly fumes of ether filtering through the crack under the door.

(Roald went to see the Matron, who prodded his stomach while he yelped and moaned ...)

Within an hour, the doctor arrived and he went through the same prodding and poking and I did my yelping at what I thought were the proper times. Then he put a thermometer in my mouth.

'Hmm,' he said. 'It reads normal. Let me feel your stomach once more.'

'Owch!' I screamed when he touched the vital spot.

The doctor went away with the Matron. The Matron returned half an hour later and said, 'The Headmaster has telephoned your mother and she's coming to fetch you this afternoon.'

I didn't answer her. I just lay there trying to look very ill, but my heart was singing out with all sorts of wonderful songs of praise and joy.

(Arriving home, Roald was taken immediately to see Dr Dunbar.)

He himself sat down behind his desk and fixed me with a penetrating but not unkindly eye. 'You're faking, aren't you?' he said.

'How do you know?' I blurted out.

'Because your stomach is soft and perfectly normal,' he answered. 'If you had had an inflammation down there, the stomach would have been hard and rigid. It's quite easy to tell.'

I kept silent.

'I expect you're homesick,' he said.

I nodded miserably.

'Everyone is at first,' he said. 'You have to stick it out. And don't blame your mother for sending you away to boarding school. She insisted you were too young to go, but it was I who persuaded her it was the right thing to do. Life is tough, and the sooner you learn how to cope with it, the better for you.'

'What will you tell the school?' I asked him, trembling.

'I'll say you had a very severe infection of the stomach which I am curing with pills,' he answered smiling. 'It will mean that you must stay home for three more days. But promise me you won't try anything like this again ...'

Roald Dahl

DEAD FAMOUS:

*Sofie decided to send Roald to St Peter's, a boys' boarding school with about 150 pupils. St Peter's sat on a hill overlooking the seaside town of Weston-super-Mare on the opposite side of the Bristol Channel from Roald's home in Wales. On the first floor of the school were six dormitories – where the boys were supposed to sleep. On the ground floor were six classrooms – where they weren't.

Many of Roald's books feature a kind of undeclared war between adults (usually teachers) and children. The adults make up all the rules to suit themselves, just like the evil headmistress, Miss Trunchbull, does in Roald's book *Matilda*. The children in Trunchbull's school think of themselves as brave soldiers fighting for their very survival every single day. Looking back, it's pretty certain that Roald's feeling of constant warfare with teachers began during his time at his new school – St Peter's.

OFF TO SCHOOL

When the first day of the autumn term arrived, Roald and his mother set off from Cardiff across the sea to Weston-super-Mare. They travelled on one of the regular paddle-steamers that chugged across the bay. Roald was allowed to bring a large trunk for his clothes, and a smaller wooden box, called a tuck box, to keep his personal belongings in.

Sofie dropped Roald off at school and, detecting that mothers were not welcome, wisely beat a hasty retreat. As his mother's taxi disappeared through the school gates, Roald started to cry. If he'd known the kind of torture that lay in store, he might have saved his tears for later.

It was the first time Roald had ever been away from his family overnight. And this wasn't just overnight – he wasn't going to see them for weeks and weeks! How would he survive? When he climbed into bed that night, Roald made sure he went to sleep facing in the direction of home. Not much comfort, but what's a boy to do? Well, actually, quite a lot.

It was no surprise that the new boy Roald came down with a terrible disease: homesickness. Within a few weeks of the start of term, Roald's devious and cunning brain was working on a way of getting himself shipped back to the bosom of his family. Even if he had to lie to do it.

*Roald's mother

ROALD DAHL

ROALD'S MARVELLOUS MEDICAL SCAM

In the summer of that year, 1925, Roald's half-sister Ellen had suffered from appendicitis. The whole family must have been especially worried because that's what *Astri had died of five years before. Roald recalled waiting anxiously as the doctor had operated on Ellen on the nursery table. (Yes, I know this is all happening less than a hundred years ago and that's really not very long, but doctors really used to arrive at people's houses and perform operations in their own homes.)

The operation was successful and Ellen was fine, but all this had given Roald an idea for escaping from school.

Before he would be sent home, however, Roald had to convince the mountainous Matron that something was really wrong.

Thanks to his half-sister, young Roald knew exactly what the symptoms of appendicitis were, AND how to fake them. He let out a yelp of pain when the matron touched what he knew was just the right spot on his stomach. Then Roald performed the same scam on the school doctor. It worked. A few hours later, and Roald was on the paddle-steamer heading for home to be reunited with his mother. He was so happy he had to keep reminding himself to look miserable. (Well, he was supposed to be ill!)

Of course the very first thing Mrs Dahl did was to take her sickly son to the local quack, Dr Dunbar. It took him about one tenth of a second to spot what the others hadn't – Roald was faking it. If the doctor told the headmaster at St Peter's, then Roald knew he'd be in dead trouble. Luckily for Roald, the doctor took pity on him. He made Roald promise never to fake an illness again. In return, the doc told the school Roald had a stomach infection and would need three days' rest at home.

*Roald's eldest sister

Andrew Donkin

John Lennon

John Lennon was one of the Beatles, the most successful band so far in the history of pop music. Things happened to him that most people can only dream about: he became a pop star in his twenties, he played guitar, wrote songs and sang to vast audiences — and he became very rich. Yet, success and fame did not always make him happy. John always seemed to be searching for something more.

Hero or villain?

To many young people, Lennon was a hero. They admired him for his music, for being rebellious and for his campaigns for peace and other causes. However he also behaved foolishly at times, took harmful drugs, broke the law and upset his friends. Few of his fans knew much about the private side of this famous man. To them, he was just John, one of the 'Fab Four' — the Beatles.

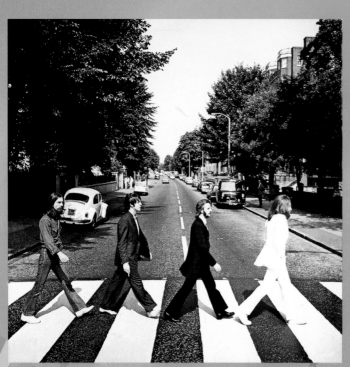

Beatlemania

While at art college in the late 1950s, John had formed a band called the Quarrymen, with some of his friends. In 1960, he gave up his college course and concentrated on becoming a musician. The band changed its name to the Beatles, and they set out hopefully on their musical career. In 1962, they released their first single, 'Love Me Do'. It got to number 17 in the charts. The Beatles were on their way!

In June 1963 the band appeared on television in their own series. By November they were on stage in London, singing in front of the royal family. John and fellow Beatle Paul McCartney were compared favourably with great music composers of the past. Fans mobbed them whenever they appeared. A new word was invented to describe the craziness: 'Beatlemania'. For the next two years, every record the Beatles made was a hit.

A hard day's night

In 1964 the Beatles started work on their first film, *A Hard Day's Night*, which was hugely successful. John and the others were working so hard they scarcely knew what time it was - the title of the film probably summed up what it felt like! In 1964 John also wrote and illustrated a book of humorous poetry and stories, *In His Own Write*, followed in 1965 by another called *A Spaniard in the Works*. Both were best-sellers.

Help!

But being so famous and popular brought its own troubles, and John was having problems with his marriage and with the band. The concerts in front of thousands of screaming fans felt like freak shows. No one could hear the music, so what was the point? "The only reason to be Beatles is to make music, not just to be in a circus," John explained sadly. Their last public concert was in America in August 1966, and the band finally broke up in 1970.

Back to work

In 1969 John had started making records on his own. One of his first was 'Give Peace a Chance'. He spoke out for peace and for civil rights, with his new wife, Yoko Ono. Over the next ten years he spent much of his time in the USA, living far more quietly than he had when he was one of the Beatles. Then, tragically, on 8 December 1980, he was shot dead in a New York street by a man claiming to be one of his fans.

Key dates

1940 **John Lennon is born in Liverpool.**
1960 **The 'Beatles' are formed and play in Hamburg.**
1962 **The Beatles have their first chart success.**
1968 **John marries Yoko Ono.**
1970 **The Beatles break up.**
1980 **John Lennon is murdered in New York.**

BOB MARLEY

- Full name – Robert Nesta Marley

- Born on 6 February 1945 in Nine Mile – small mountain village in Jamaica

- Mother was Cedella Booker – 18-year-old black girl

- Father was Norval Marley – 50-year-old white naval captain

- At age 12, moved to Kingston with his mother

- Saw little of his father as a child

- He loved football

- Lived in poor district of Kingston in a small concrete house

- Made up music with his friend Bunny – on sardine-can guitar

- Left school at 14 and became apprentice at local welder's

- 1964: formed a band called the Wailers with two friends, Bunny and Tosh

- Band performed typical Jamaican music called 'reggae'

- Strong commitment to Rastafarian religion – wore hair in dreadlocks

- Wrote songs about religion, politics and social issues

- 1971: signed to Island Records label

- The Wailers were one of the most popular reggae bands of the 1970s

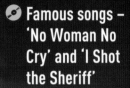

- Famous songs – 'No Woman No Cry' and 'I Shot the Sheriff'

- 'He was a great lyric writer, a musical genius and a leader of men' (Eric Clapton, rock star)

- 1974: Wailers split up

- 1978: shot by a would-be assassin when he spoke out against gang warfare

- Marley got cancer and lost his hair – but kept it as a wig!

- Died of cancer on 11 May, 1981

- Buried in Nine Mile village with his bible and his guitar

- Former home in Kingston is now a museum

- He is Jamaica's most famous son

FACTS, FACTS, FACTS: identifying and using the structure and features of non-chronological reports.

Unit 2

THE SECRET LIFE OF BUGS

The world is full of tiny creatures. Some are just big enough to see; others are visible only under powerful microscopes. Although most of these bugs are harmless to humans, some can be real pests, and a few can be extremely dangerous. On these three pages you can read firstly about bugs all around us, secondly about bugs on us, and thirdly about bugs in us!

Dust mite

DUST MITE DANGER

Dust mites live wherever we do, feeding on flakes of dead skin that fall from our bodies. As with humans, what goes into dust mites later comes out too. Consequently they leave behind particles of excrement, which we then breathe in. These particles can sometimes have a bad effect: making us short of breath, even causing asthma attacks.

BEWARE OF BLOOD SUCKERS

Fleas in your fur

Besides the bugs that feed on our dead skin, there are others – like the flea – that suck our fresh blood. There are about 1600 different types of flea. Many specialise in biting just one type of hairy creature: cats, dogs, rabbits – or us. Fleas come and go for their meals, jumping distances up to 100 times their own body length.

Hungry head lice

Whereas fleas are energetic bloodsuckers, head lice are not. These six-legged bugs cling on for dear life to individual hairs; they cannot be washed off as easily as fleas. They do little but feed – sucking blood from our scalps every 3 to 6 hours. They also lay eggs, called nits, which hatch into the next generation of head lice. In a 30-day lifetime, one louse can stick as many as 300 eggs to the hairs on our heads.

Head louse

GERMS OUT TO GET US

Mites, fleas and lice make our lives difficult; tinier bugs known as micro-organisms can actually kill us. Another name for these microscopic creatures is 'microbes', while another still is 'germs'. They invade our bodies through contact with other infected people, or if we do not keep ourselves clean. There are two main groups of germs that cause human diseases: bacteria and viruses.

Bacteria are absolutely everywhere – around us and on us – but most of them are quite safe. In fact, they do all kinds of useful jobs. The bad bacteria are the infectious ones that get in through a cut or via a body opening. Then they multiply amazingly fast, causing diseases like tetanus which can kill.

Viruses are even smaller than bacteria but can be even more deadly. Once inside, a virus will attack a single cell (that is the smallest complete working part in our bodies). It forces the cell to make more and more viruses until the cell dies of exhaustion. Then the new viruses move on to infect other cells.

GERM WARFARE

There are many different types of virus infection. They range from common colds and flu to the rare Ebola, which can destroy most of our blood vessels in just 7 days. Luckily, our white blood cells wage war on many germs and overcome them. They also make 'antibodies', to stop us getting a repeat infection. So we never get ill from exactly the same kind of cold more than once. Not so luckily, there are well over 100 different kinds of common cold virus!

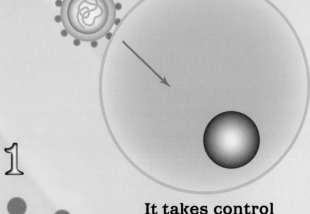

It takes control
of a cell

It makes the
cell produce
more viruses

A simple virus particle
looks like this

This is how a
virus goes about
its dirty work.
The pictures
shows you
something that
would normally
only be seen by a
scientist with a
very powerful
microscope in a
laboratory.

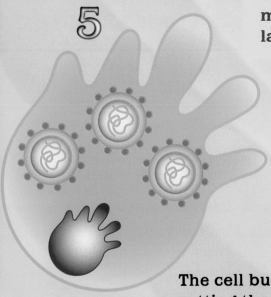

The cell bursts,
setting the
viruses free

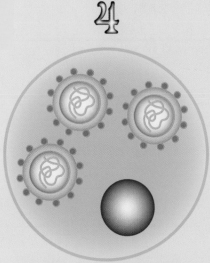

The cell fills with
new viruses

NOW will you Wash your Hands?

If you ever prepare food without washing your hands first, these pictures may help you to change your ways. Every speck represents bacteria which can cause food poisoning. To the naked eye, the hands look clean, but actions like handling raw chicken or wiping your hands on a dishcloth can coat them with deadly germs.

A national survey

A survey carried out during National Food Safety week found that, although most people are aware of the names of major bugs, like salmonella and e.coli, they don't realize how important it is to keep their hands clean.

- 42% of the 2,000 people interviewed did not always wash their hands after contact with pets, and more than half did not wash them before eating.

- A quarter of men and 17% of women did not always wash their hands before preparing food.

- 31% of men and 17% of women did not wash their hands after going to the lavatory.

RAW MEAT

16

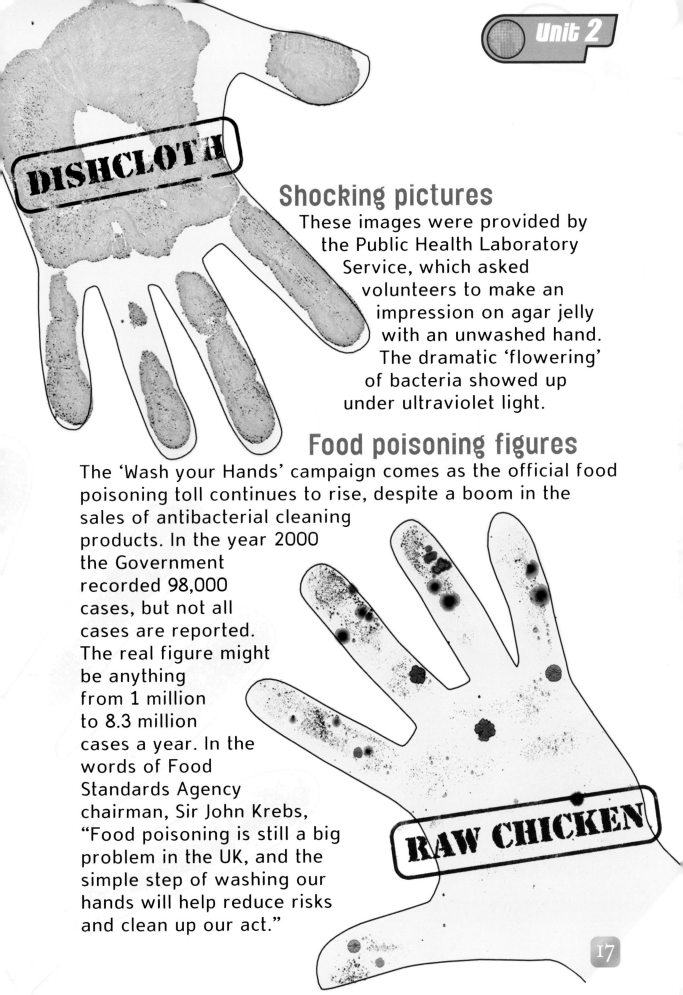

DISHCLOTH

Shocking pictures

These images were provided by the Public Health Laboratory Service, which asked volunteers to make an impression on agar jelly with an unwashed hand. The dramatic 'flowering' of bacteria showed up under ultraviolet light.

Food poisoning figures

The 'Wash your Hands' campaign comes as the official food poisoning toll continues to rise, despite a boom in the sales of antibacterial cleaning products. In the year 2000 the Government recorded 98,000 cases, but not all cases are reported. The real figure might be anything from 1 million to 8.3 million cases a year. In the words of Food Standards Agency chairman, Sir John Krebs, "Food poisoning is still a big problem in the UK, and the simple step of washing our hands will help reduce risks and clean up our act."

RAW CHICKEN

Theatres in Shakespeare's Time

William Shakespeare lived from 1564 to 1616. During the last twenty years of his life he wrote, acted in and directed plays at London's theatres. This was a Golden Age for theatre-goers. Thirty-eight of Shakespeare's plays have survived; so have 200 more by other stage writers like Ben Jonson, Thomas Kyd and Christopher Marlowe. Many of these plays are still performed for audiences today.

William Shakespeare, whose plays have been popular ever since he wrote them, 400 years ago.

The New Outdoor Playhouses

Before Shakespeare's time London had no proper theatres. Instead, bands of actors put on plays in the courtyards of inns or other open spaces. Sometimes they travelled around the country, performing in one town after another. Then in 1567 a large wooden theatre called the Red Lion was built in London. Soon there were others: the Swan, the Rose and the Globe. People flocked to afternoon performances at these open-air 'playhouses'. Some sat to watch, some stood; and some moved around picking pockets! Over 2000 people crammed in for each show.

Indoor Theatres

Compared with the Globe, central London's Blackfriars theatre was far more luxurious; consequently it cost six times as much to sit and watch a play there. This new indoor theatre measured just 46 x 66ft (13.8 x 19.8m), so only 700 spectators could be let in at a time. The stage was lit by hanging candles, and it was easier to put on other special effects there than out in the open.

Besides watching plays here, England's richest people also saw shows at the royal court. Both Queen Elizabeth I (who reigned from 1558 to 1603) and King James I (1603–25) loved being entertained by actors. Between 1603 and 1616, an acting company called the King's Men performed almost 200 times at court.

Theatre scene from the film 'Shakespeare in Love', 1998.

Seventeenth-Century Celebrities

A leading member of the King's Men was William Shakespeare. Even in his own lifetime, he was famous for his writing skills. As well as history plays he wrote fantasies, light-hearted love stories and comedies, while some of his greatest work was terrifying or deeply moving.

Shakespeare was lucky that stars like Richard Burbage and Will Kempe also belonged to the King's Men. They were the celebrities of the time, and theatre-goers often came just to see them perform. Shakespeare therefore made sure he wrote parts in his plays that showed off their special talents.

Will Kempe, a very gifted comic actor, had two claims to fame. Firstly, he starred in many of Shakespeare's plays. Secondly, he once danced 140 miles in 9 days – all the way from London to Norwich!

Shakespeare's Globe

The Globe

London's Globe Theatre, home of the King's Men acting company, was built just south of the River Thames in 1599. A visitor from Switzerland wrote this about one of its first shows: 'After dinner at about 2 o'clock, I went with my party across the water. In the straw-thatched house we saw a play about the Roman Emperor Julius Caesar. It was very pleasantly performed, with approximately 15 characters.' The play he saw must have been Shakespeare's 'Julius Caesar'.

An exterior view of the Globe, based on an original drawing from 1616 – not to scale!

New Globe from the Old World

A new copy of the Globe theatre now stands south of the river in London. In many ways, going to see plays there today is the same as in Shakespeare's time. But in other ways, it is not! Modern showings of Shakespeare's plays are much less rowdy affairs than the originals were!

A modern-day photo of the interior of the reconstructed Globe.

An interior view of the Swan theatre, based on a sixteenth-century drawing.

These covered seats, or galleries, were for richer spectators; but there were dangers even here. From 1592 to 1594 London was hit by a terrible infectious disease called the plague. Germs spread rapidly wherever people are packed together; therefore all the playhouses had to close down.

Flag shows a play will be on that afternoon. There were no evening shows, since there was no way of lighting up the open-air theatre.

No background scenery

Boy-actors, not women, usually took the female parts in the plays.

Splendid costumes, which may have been inherited by servants of rich masters, and then sold to the acting company

Space reserved for 'groundlings' (spectators who stood on the ground). They cheered and booed the action like fans at a modern football match. In 1597 the Lord Mayor of London called these poorer play-goers: 'thieves, horse-stealers and other idle and dangerous persons.'

Special effects. Here, a bladder of pig's blood, hidden under the actor's costume, has been stabbed and blood is spurting out! In 1613, during a Shakespeare play at the Globe, a small cannon was fired. It set the thatched roof on fire, and the whole theatre burned down and had to be rebuilt. Amazingly, no one was killed.

Unit 3

HOT OFF THE PRESS: looking at the features of magazine articles and newspaper reports, and thinking about bias; learning how to present a newspaper report.

RUBBISH: DOWN IN THE DUMPS

The day that primitive man first threw away a broken arrow-head was the day that we became a throw-away society. And that was all right, because the Earth could absorb our rubbish. What did not rot down, remained to provide fascinating insights into how we once lived. However, as our society has evolved, so has our rubbish. Modern materials and chemicals mean that we now generate kinds and quantities of rubbish that can't be absorbed. This new kind of rubbish is, at best, unpleasant and can even be dangerous. For sure, there will be no shortage of artefacts for the archaeologists of the future – landfill sites will provide treasure troves of them! This may be the only good thing to be said about our main method of waste disposal.

Our bad habit of throwing things away when we have done with them has created a mountain of rubbish. Much of our waste is big stuff! Cars, tyres, fridges, etc., take up a vast amount of space. For years we have tipped our rubbish into disused quarries, gravel pits and mine workings. But although there are 2,264 landfill sites in England and Wales alone, this is no longer enough. New sites are still being opened up all over the country. One of those sites could be just around the corner from you! Eighty per cent of us live within one mile of a tip. Consequently, eighty per cent of us may have experienced some of the problems.

THE PROBLEMS WITH RUBBISH DISPOSAL

✳ First, there's the sheer quantity of the stuff.

✳ Secondly, there is the smell. Even after a few days, household rubbish like those old tea bags, fish skins and half-eaten takeaways in your wheelie bin smell decidedly 'off'. Multiply the smell of your bin by whatever lurks inside all the other thousands of bins in town, and you can imagine things getting a bit whiffy.

✳ Then there's the danger and noise as heavy lorries ply to and fro carrying anything from household refuse to hazardous industrial waste.

✳ Also, never underestimate the noise, dirt and nuisance from those wheeling, screaming flocks of seagulls that look for food on the sites.

✳ Increasingly, pollution is a major cause for concern. As the rubbish rots down, dangerous substances can leak into the water supply and the farmland all around. Chemicals can combine to make poisonous gases which then escape into the atmosphere. Consequently, houses close to landfill sites are often difficult to sell and lose value.

✳ What is even more worrying is that recent reports suggest that babies born in such areas are more likely to have health problems.

SO WHAT'S TO BE DONE?

We need to reduce the quantity of rubbish by composting biodegradable materials, and by recycling discarded items where we can. Incineration is another possibility, but it can create fresh hazards. One exciting new idea is to turn our problems to our advantage, by using the methane gas produced by landfill sites to generate electricity. Yesterday's pollution could become today's source of renewable energy. Perhaps this may be a way forward?

PACKAGING: The Big Cover-up

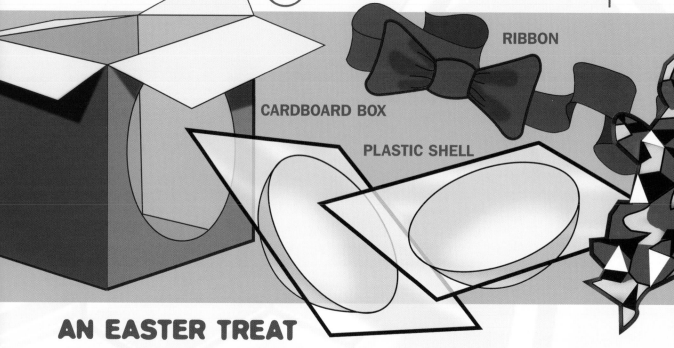

RIBBON

CARDBOARD BOX

PLASTIC SHELL

AN EASTER TREAT

The package looks exciting. Let's unwrap it. First open the cardboard box. Now lift the contents from the moulded, clear plastic container. Next, undo the ribbon and peel off the foil. At last – chocolate! But there's more inside: a cellophane bag containing six individually wrapped chocolates. No, this isn't a game of Pass the Parcel: we've just unwrapped a typical Easter Egg and its contents– all eleven layers of it!

The multi-million-dollar packaging industry comes in for a great deal of criticism for over-packaging such as this. Its throw-away products are a huge burden on the environment, causing mountains of waste and draining unsustainable resources.

Yet, aren't most of us guilty of over-packaging from time to time? What about that birthday present? It was

already packaged when we bought it, but we wrapped it in attractive gift-wrap, tied it with ribbon and popped it into a trendy gift bag with a matching tag. Consequently, we too added to the rubbish mountain.

WHAT DO WE REALLY WANT?

This then, is the dilemma. We do need some packaging, but only

What we want is a pack that protects its contents from the point of production to the point of consumption; a pack that uses the minimum amount of materials and

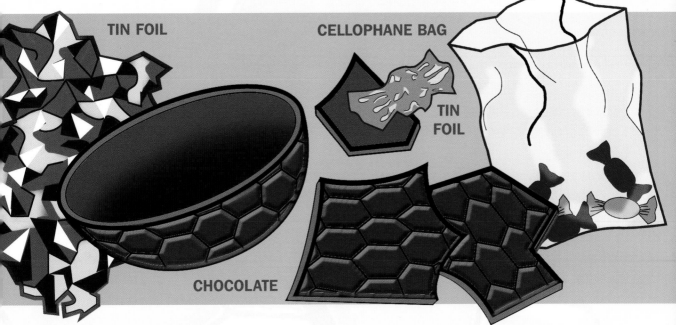

TIN FOIL

CELLOPHANE BAG

TIN FOIL

CHOCOLATE

enough to keep the contents in good condition and fit for their purpose. How can we sift out the unnecessary marketing glitz that gives the product the gotta-have-it factor?

Food and drink packaging attracts the most criticism with its glass jars and bottles, cans and aerosols, foil containers, cardboard boxes, paper bags and plastic, plastic, plastic! Do we really need it all?

We've come to expect that our food and drink will be fresh, that it will be clean and that it will be in good condition. Therefore, we certainly need some form of packaging. However, we also expect this packaging to be environmentally friendly. What do we mean by that?

energy to manufacture; and one that leaves the least amount of waste.

What are the packaging manufacturers doing to achieve these requirements? The increasing demand for environmentally friendly packaging materials means that they must respond or lose their customers. But this is an industry where 'intelligent' robots can produce plastic drink bottles at a rate of 60,000 per hour in factories that look like something from sci-fi films. It's an industry that can make bags for frozen burgers that will open themselves when the food inside is cooked! With such state-of-the-art technology, surely they can crack the environmental problems?

SOME NEW IDEAS

Nevertheless, it would seem that the packaging industry overall is getting the message. So far it has come up with two types of self-destructive materials manufactured from potato starch and maize, which can replace the plastics used for fruit and vegetable trays. Unlike other plastics, these can be composted. Moreover, in an effort to relieve the pressure on landfill sites, it has also devised a collapsible plastic bottle that folds in on itself, reducing its area by 60%. Each bottle carries a secret message that is only revealed when the bottle is folded up. Clever!

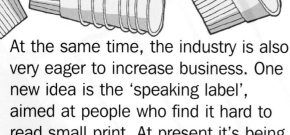

At the same time, the industry is also very eager to increase business. One new idea is the 'speaking label', aimed at people who find it hard to read small print. At present it's being trialled on medicine packaging, where a microchip embedded in the label will 'tell' patients their medication dosage! (Whatever will the humble baked bean tin say in the future?)

On the other hand, we have heard that a very well known supermarket wants to display one of its first 'Value' baked bean tins in its head office. Furthermore it's offering £500 to anyone who has one. Not a bad deal for something that cost 17p only ten years ago! So, perhaps we should hang on to our packaging after all – it may all become collectors' items in the future!

THE DAILY PRESS

12TH August 1999   50p

TOTAL ECLIPSE!
Darkness descends at midday

By John Cansfield

A SHADOW descended over Britain yesterday as the Moon eclipsed the Sun for the last time in the present millennium. Millions stopped work to view the dramatic events and the National Grid experienced its biggest ever surge in power as people returned to work. A million people crowded into the county of Cornwall to get the best views. Billions more witnessed the eclipse worldwide as it travelled past Newfoundland across heavily populated areas in Europe and over Pakistan and India. It was the most watched eclipse of all time.

It all started at 10.30 a.m. our time as early risers on Signal Hill in Newfoundland saw two sunrises close together. The 70-mile-wide path of the eclipse then raced across the Atlantic Ocean, chased by 200 passengers on board the supersonic jet Concorde. It first crossed the British mainland at Penzance in Cornwall at 11.11 a.m. on 11th August. Streetlights switched themselves on as the sun began to vanish. Swallows dashed to the trees believing it to be dusk. The air grew chilly as the skies darkened and observers felt a strong gust of wind spring up. The well-known astronomer Patrick Hughes said: 'It was an awe-inspiring but eerie experience. The fall in the light and temperature was remarkable.'

As a partial eclipse reached the rest of Britain, judges and barristers in London left the Old Bailey courts for a special 30-minute 'eclipse adjournment', though the people on trial were not allowed out. Thousands of office workers thronged bridges across the Thames or watched from boats. The normally packed Underground was deserted and eerily quiet. Prisoners in Manchester were allowed into the exercise yard to watch as the skies grew dark.

Across Europe, the eclipse continued to amaze observers and confuse local wildlife. On the Black Sea coast of Romania, confused fish swimming in the shallows were caught by tourists with their bare hands. In Rome, the Pope shortened his weekly meeting with visitors so no one would miss the eclipse. In the Indian city of Allahabad, thousands of Hindus bathed in the sacred waters of the Ganges during the eclipse, believing this would lead to reincarnation as Brahmin, the highest social caste.

Despite worries about eye safety beforehand, there were few reported incidents of people damaging their sight when watching the eclipse. The public had been warned by experts not to gaze directly at the sun without protection and not to use ordinary sunglasses. Most people used specially designed protective glasses to look at the sun. Others improvised devices such as welders' masks or viewed the eclipse reflected in water.

The next total eclipse of the Sun in Britain will be at 5p.m. on 23rd September, 2090, when West Cornwall will again be the best place to see it. But would-be eclipse-watchers need to remember to book their viewing points early. Some hotels in Cornwall had been fully booked for yesterday's eclipse since 1991.

Cornwall was the most popular hotspot yesterday for eclipse watchers

Unit 4   A MATTER OF OPINION: learning to recognize the features of discussion texts, building a bank of useful words, and constructing a balanced argument.

Organic is Best — Or Is It?

Organic food has become more popular in the past few years and as demand for it has risen, so a wider range of organic foods has become available in the shops. But what *is* organic food and is it better for us than non-organic produce?

FOR: Going organic

To be an organic farmer you must grow or rear food without using chemical fertilisers and pesticides and other artificial treatments. Instead, organic farmers put back the nutrients taken out of the soil by the plants they grow, by dressing it with manure from plant-eating farm animals.

People who produce organic food say that although it costs a bit more, it is worth the extra money. This is because they believe their food not only *tastes* better, but *is* better, since they claim it contains more vitamins and minerals than non-organic food. They point out that their food is free from traces of poisonous chemicals that are found in about 25% of non-organic foods.

Organic farmers also believe that the way they rear their animals is better than the conventional way. They feel their animals lead a more natural life in less crowded conditions, and are spared the regular doses of antibiotics and other medicines which non-organic farmers give to their animals, whether they are ill or not.

Furthermore, the environment benefits from organic farming methods, since these do not involve the use of the artificial pesticides and herbicides which harm wildlife and pollute natural water supplies.

People concerned about animal welfare and the environment have no doubt that organic is the better choice.

AGAINST: Going cheap

Over the years, farmers have been encouraged by the government to find ways of producing cheap and plentiful food. To do this, they have had to move away from traditional organic methods of farming, towards the more intensive farming we see today. As a result, people have got used to finding, and expecting, inexpensive food in the shops.

Non-organic farmers argue that if people continue to want cheap food, then chemicals and factory farming methods will be have to be used. In their opinion, the amounts of chemical residue found in some non-organic foods are too small to be harmful. They point out that the animals they rear are safe, warm, well fed and free from disease.

They might also mention that, although it is generally thought that organic means completely free of chemicals, this is not so, as *some* chemicals are licensed for use in organic farming.

Furthermore, organic does not always mean healthier. This is particularly true of some processed organic foods which may contain more fat and sugar than their non-organic equivalent!

There is also the issue of 'food miles': a high proportion of organic food is produced abroad, then flown hundreds or thousands of miles to UK supermarkets. The polluting effects of the air transport should also be taken into account.

At the moment only 3% of UK farmland is farmed organically and the majority of the organic foods you see in the shops actually comes from abroad.

Organic or non-organic?

So, is organic food better for us? Is it better for the environment? On the one hand, organic farmers claim their produce is healthier, while on the other, the Food Standards Agency says there is no scientific proof that organic food is any more safe or nutritious than non-organic!

Whoever is right, the reality is that most people still choose to buy non-organic food. Is this because they believe such food is safe and nutritious? Or is it because organic food is usually more expensive and they do not want to pay the extra? True enough if more people were to buy organic food and more UK farmers were to grow it, then the price would come down. But in the end, it's up to you. Organic or non-organic? What do you think?

COMPUTERS ARE BAD FOR YOU!

Yes, it's true! Computers *are* bad for you because using computers can damage your health.

Every day, millions of people spend time working or playing on computers. Most of them probably don't think twice about the effect this *could* be having on their health. However, the matter is now so serious, that one report has estimated that personal injury, associated with computer use, *could* be costing UK businesses in the region of half a billion pounds a year!

Many of the health problems associated with using computers are due to prolonged usage. For example, some people find they get pain or stiffness in their neck, back and shoulders from sitting in the same position at their computer terminal for a long time. Others find that computers can cause problems with their eyes. They may complain that they have tired, dry eyes or a headache from focusing on the screen for many hours.

Now I know what that label means.

PC PLAN

WARNING: COMPUTERS CAN SERIOUSLY DAMAGE YOUR HEALTH.

But even worse, people can develop a painful condition known as RSI, or Repetitive Strain Injury. This is triggered by the repetitive hand, wrist and arm movements involved when using a keyboard, mouse or joystick for hours on end. It causes inflammation of the tendons in the hands and pain or discomfort in the fingers, arms and wrists.

Some people can also become worryingly addicted to their computer, spending hours at a time playing computer games or surfing the net, so that they end up losing social skills, preferring the company of their computer to mixing with other people.

And of course, there is the mental anguish and stress that people suffer when they accidentally delete a vital piece of work! Or when their computer is attacked by a virus! Or it crashes!

So perhaps it is time that computers came with some sort of government health warning. At the very least, for the sake of our health, we should be thinking about limiting the time we spend sitting at a computer!

Village Life

Two hundred years ago, most people in the UK lived in villages, but now the majority of people live in towns and cities. If you live in a village, would you swap village life for the attractions of town, or are you happy where you are?

FOR A perfect place

I just love living in our village. It's so quiet and peaceful compared to a town or city. There is some noise from cars here, but none of the smelly pollution that comes with the really heavy traffic and factories that you get in towns.

I love the fact that our village is surrounded by fields and woodland and open countryside, where I can take my dog, ride my bike and play with my friends.

I also like going to the friendly village school. It's so small it only has two classrooms – one for the infants and one for the juniors – and if there is a school outing, we all go! It's right in the centre of our village and it only takes me two minutes to walk there.

Our village is a friendly place. Everyone knows everyone else, and we look after each other! When new people come, everyone knows it. There is hardly any crime, so I am allowed a lot more freedom to play out on my own than perhaps I would be in a more built-up area.

I'm only sad that I'll have to move away when I'm grown up because houses here are getting so expensive that I won't be able to afford to live here.

Village houses are increasingly being bought by people who commute to work in nearby towns.

Is It For You?

Alternatively, if you live in a built-up area, would moving to a village be your dream come true or your worst nightmare?

Here, children from the same village offer opposing views.

AGAINST Get me out of here!

I wish I lived in a town or city. This place is just too quiet for my liking. Nothing ever happens here. You see the same old faces, day in and day out, and because everyone knows everyone else, they also know all your business!

There really isn't anything for young people to do around here. I'd prefer to live somewhere where there are new people to meet and where there is a lot more going on. I mean, can you imagine what it is like, living in a place where you can't get a signal on your mobile phone and there are no cinemas, no cafés, no sports facilities, no clothes shops?

If our family had a car it wouldn't be so bad, because we could go into town when we wanted. You really need a car if you live out here – it's hopeless getting anywhere otherwise. There *are* buses, but only two a day and nothing after six o'clock at night!

At least when I go to secondary school next year it will be in town. But the downside is, I'll have to get up very early as it takes a good hour for the coach to get there by the time it has picked everybody up.

I can't wait until I'm grown up. I'm looking forward to living somewhere – anywhere – more lively and interesting than here!

Village life obviously isn't for everyone! Would it suit you?

You can't even go to the library after school because it only comes once a week – in a van!

A PROPOSAL FOR A NEW FITNESS CLUB

INSHAPE Fitness Clubs has applied for permission to build a new facility near your village. The club will be built on the site of the current cricket pavilion and recreation ground.

State-of-the-art facilities would be offered for members only, including:
SWIMMING POOL ● GYM ● SUN BEDS
BADMINTON AND SQUASH COURTS ● SAUNA

THE FOLLOWING BENEFITS WOULD BE BROUGHT TO YOUR VILLAGE:

- New coffee shop and bar
- Parking for up to 75 cars
- Employment for local people
- Membership discount for local residents
- Children's holiday activities for members.

WE THINK YOU'LL AGREE THIS DEVELOPMENT IS BADLY NEEDED BECAUSE:

- The nearest facilities are currently 20 miles away.
- Without a car villagers cannot go to evening and weekend sessions.
- Children have no indoor facilities at present.
- People from nearby villages would be attracted.

WRITE TO YOUR LOCAL COUNCIL IF YOU SUPPORT OUR EXCITING NEW PROPOSAL TO ENHANCE YOUR VILLAGE LIFE AND IMPROVE YOUR HEALTH. SHOW YOUR SUPPORT AT THE PLANNING INQUIRY

TO WHOM IT MAY CONCERN: looking at different kinds of formal writing, recognizing its features, and learning when to use it.

Unit 5

Larkrise Residential Centre

SAFETY NOTICE

To ensure the safety of all visitors, it is requested that the following rules are observed:

INSIDE THE BUILDING

1. Walk quietly in the dormitories and dining areas.
2. The bottom bunk beds may not be used by children over 1.5m tall.
3. Mobile phones are prohibited in submarines and spacecraft.
4. Do not enter the swimming pool without adult supervision.

OUTSIDE THE BUILDING

1. Follow the instructions of Centre staff at all times.
2. Keep to the marked pathways.
3. The rainforest survival trail is out of bounds after dusk.
4. Sharp objects are not permitted near the inflatable speedboats.
5. On no account enter the loch unless in a submarine.

Larkrise Residential Centre

HEALTH QUESTIONNAIRE

Name ☐☐☐☐☐☐☐☐☐☐☐☐☐☐☐☐☐☐☐☐☐☐

Age ☐☐   Height ☐☐☐   Date of Birth ☐☐☐☐☐☐☐☐

Does your child need to take any medicines regularly? [Y][N]

Has your child been in contact with any infectious diseases in the past two weeks? (e.g. measles, malaria, etc.) [Y][N]

Does your child suffer from any of the following:
Travel sickness? [Y][N]   Eczema? [Y][N]   Fear of poisonous snakes? [Y][N]

Is your child allergic to any of the following: Chocolate? [Y][N] Vegetables? [Y][N] Margarine? [Y][N]

Does your child have any special dietary needs?
Please specify ☐☐☐☐☐☐☐☐☐☐☐☐☐☐☐☐☐☐☐☐☐☐☐☐☐☐☐☐☐☐☐☐☐☐☐

Is your child medically fit to take part in the following:
a) White-water rafting? [Y][N]   b) Space travel? [Y][N]   c) Underwater exploration? [Y][N]

Please add any other relevant information overleaf or on a separate sheet.

Signature of parent/carer _____ Date _____

The Official Constitution of The Greenies Club

- The club shall hereafter be known as The Greenies.
- The club shall be run by a Leader who will be elected by a majority of the other members.
- The Leader shall appoint a secretary, who will be responsible for all membership applications and the administration of the club.
- The secretary shall appoint a treasurer who will be responsible for all the club's money.
- Members shall pay a subscription of 10p a week to the treasurer.
- New members must be proposed by an existing member of the aforementioned club.
- Those wishing to become members can only be admitted with the agreement of all existing members.
- Meetings shall take place in the garden shed on Tuesdays commencing at 4pm.
- Members shall wear an item of green clothing at all times.
- Members shall eat an item of green food every day.
- Full membership shall be attained at a ceremony at which the entrant repeats The Greenies' Pledge.
- The club badge must be worn at all times.
- The membership card must be brought to all meetings in order to gain admission.
- Failure to abide by the rules of the club shall result in immediate expulsion.
- The motto of the club shall be *semper viridis. (*forever green)
- Membership forms may be obtained from the club secretary at the garden shed on Tuesdays.

SEMPER VIRIDIS

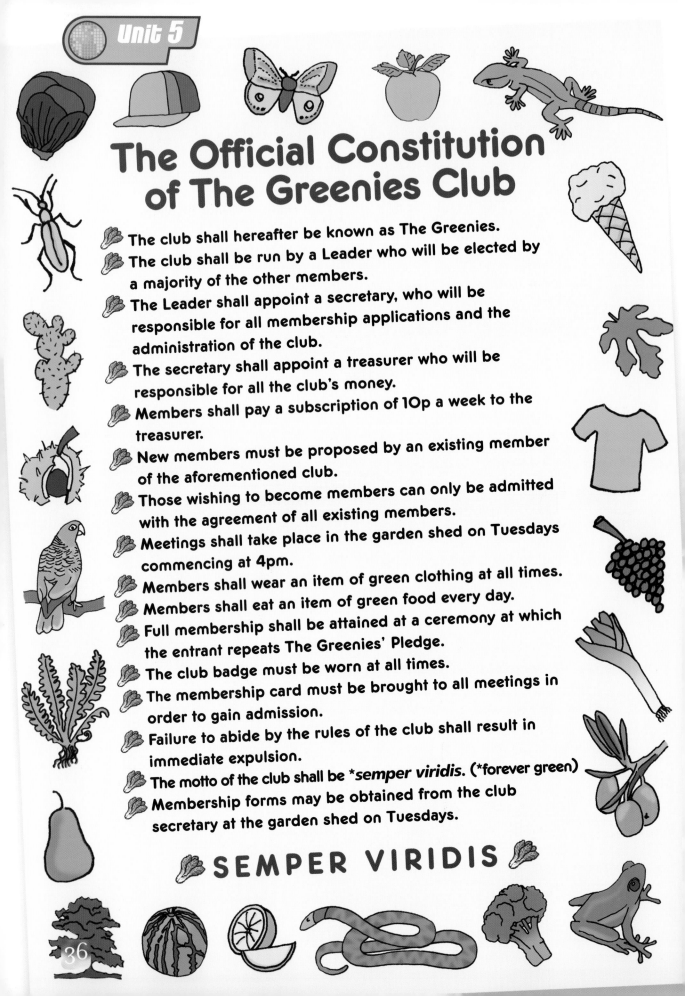

The Greenies: Membership Form

Name of applicant:................................... Age:........ Date of birth:...............

How did you hear about The Greenies?...
....

Why do you want to join The Greenies?..
....

....

What items of green clothing do you possess?...

Which of the following green foods are you prepared to eat? Tick all that apply:

- Broccoli
- Mint ice-cream
- Cucumber
- Lime jelly
- Green apples

Which of the following activities do you enjoy? Number in order of preference (1 = first choice, 5 = last, etc)

- Football
- Cycling
- Camping
- Swimming
- Gardening

In support of your application, please state anything you have done recently which has helped living things or the world around you.

....

....

Signed:................................... Date:...

Proposed by:............................. Membership number:.................................

welcome to Heathcote Zoo

A GRR . . . EAT DAY OUT!

Are you looking for a fun-filled family day out? Where better than Heathcote Zoo, where you can find something for all ages! Heathcote Zoo boasts one of the country's finest collection of animals from around the world, as well as a host of special attractions and top-class facilities.

SO MUCH TO SEE AND DO!

☆ Delight at the antics of our chattering chimps as they take their afternoon tea (twice daily)!

☆ Thrill to the spectacular performing dolphins as they show off their tricks in our purpose-built dolphinarium.

☆ Experience the humps and bumps of the camel rides (weather permitting).

FEEDING TIME!

Our welcoming café offers a wide selection of healthy, home-cooked food at exceptional prices. But that's not all: you are free to bring your own food and enjoy a relaxing picnic in our beautiful landscaped gardens. Toilets and baby changing facilities are available throughout the site. In addition to our extensive range of souvenirs, ice cream, drinks and snacks are available from the gift shop. A free land-train service is on hand to carry you around the site.

SPECIALLY FOR CHILDREN

Children are welcome to feed and stroke the animals in our unique Hands-On Area. When they want to go wild, there's the Jungle adventure playground for older children and the Clearing, where little ones can play safely. If that's not enough, your kids can also sample our brilliant bouncy castles, fantastic face painting, chuckle-a-minute children's entertainments (subject to availability) and the amazing butterfly maze.

EDUCATIONAL SERVICES

Teachers, bring your class to the zoo and liven up your lessons! We can offer fun learning opportunities through a full programme of talks and activities. Let your pupils tickle a tarantula, chat to a chinchilla or get pally with a python in our Discovery Experience. Not only that, but they can meet the keepers and talk to them about the animals they look after. We also provide a full pack of worksheets which meet all the relevant National Curriculum requirements and provide helpful suggestions for related homework tasks.

CONSERVATION AT HEATHCOTE ZOO

Our zoo is home to many animals facing extinction. The breeding programme helps to ensure the continued survival of many threatened species. By visiting our zoo you can help to save these endangered creatures.

HEATHCOTE
PROBABLY THE BEST ZOO EXPERIENCE YOU'LL EVER HAVE!

ADOPTING AN ANIMAL

Through our adoption scheme you or your school can actively help to care for endangered species and help us in our commitment to wildlife conservation.

PET CARE CENTRE

In this specially designed centre, our expert staff will teach you about the responsibilities of pet ownership. You can pick up tips about caring for popular pets such as rabbits, budgerigars, guinea pigs and hamsters.

HOW TO FIND US

We are conveniently situated just five miles west of Junction 6 of the M99. Simply follow the signs from the motorway slip road. We offer a spacious and convenient car park, with disabled access and wheelchair hire. Heathcote railway station is only five minutes' walk from the zoo entrance. Frequent buses to the zoo run from Heathcote bus station.

OPENING TIMES

We are open every day except Christmas Day, from 10am. Last admission is 3.30 p.m. in winter and 4.30 p.m. in summer.

ZOOS: ARKS OR PRISONS?

THE ZOOS' STORY

A visit to the zoo (short for zoological gardens) has been seen as a harmless family day out for well over a hundred years. Since London Zoo opened in 1867, zoos have grown from small exhibitions of unusual animals to large attractions with children's rides, entertainments, shops and cafés. Modern zoos also claim they do valuable work in education and conservation. However, campaigners for animal rights say that keeping wild animals captive for public display is wrong and should be stopped.

THE CASE FOR

Zoos argue that they provide what the public wants: to be able to see unusual animals without having to travel too far or pay too much. As well as entertainment, zoos claim they are providing educational opportunities too, as many people want their children to see the animals and learn about wildlife. Zoos

set up information boards and put on talks and displays; they also let children feed and stroke smaller animals. Most zoos offer educational resources and encourage schools to visit and study the animals.

Larger modern zoos point out that they do important research into the breeding and behaviour of animals that helps us to understand them better. They stress their role in the conservation of wildlife through breeding endangered species. Many of these are born in captivity and would not be able to survive if they were returned to the wild.

Zoo owners say that they follow strict government standards. They insist that old buildings, such as concrete enclosures for polar bears, and bear pits, have been demolished. The new accommodation is designed to be like the animals' natural environment. Some zoos have also decided not to keep larger animals such as elephants.

Modern zoos feel they are doing a valuable job and should be allowed to continue.

THE CASE AGAINST

On the other hand, critics of zoos believe that confining wild animals causes them stress and suffering, and that keeping them captive for human entertainment is outdated in the 21st century. Modern technology enables us to watch animals in the wild on television and the internet. Tourists can also travel the world to see animals in their natural habitat — properly managed, this does not interfere with their lifestyle. In zoos, animals are constantly disturbed by visitors and camera flashes.

Zoos do not educate, critics say. Although some provide useful information, people don't always read it. Also, zoo animals do not behave naturally in captivity; shows often feature animals such as elephants, seals, chimps and dolphins performing tricks they would never do in the wild.

Only a tiny minority of zoos carry out worthwhile research, according to anti-zoo groups. As far as conservation is concerned, few animals kept in zoos are actually endangered — and any that are bred in zoos would probably not survive if returned to the wild.

The growing popularity of 'hands-on' areas, where visitors can stroke, hold and feed animals has its dangers: diseases called 'zoonoses' can be transmitted between humans and animals. Even where washing facilities are provided, they may not be effective in removing harmful bacteria and viruses from the hands.

Campaigners believe that animals have a right to live as they would in the wild, and that the 'captive industry' can never provide that.

ZOOS IN THE FUTURE

There are still about 10,000 zoos across the world, although their popularity has declined in some countries. As long as governments carry on revising rules about animal welfare, zoos will be forced to keep improving their facilities. Until or unless they are banned outright, it seems that 'a day out at the zoo' will continue . . .

POWERED FLIGHT

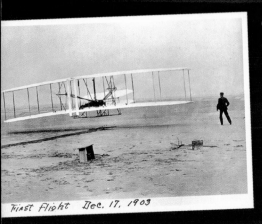

First Flight Dec. 17, 1903

On 17 December 1903 at Kitty Hawk in the USA, a flimsy biplane powered by a small petrol engine made a flight of just 12 seconds. The flight was watched by four men and a boy. The plane was piloted by Orville Wright. He and his brother Wilbur had designed and built this 'flying machine' using their skills as bicycle engineers. A new era had begun: the world's first aeroplane had flown and the age of powered flight was under way. The Wright brothers' aircraft was the first powered, controllable, heavier-than-air machine ever to fly. Up till then, the only serious flying machines had been hot-air balloons, which are lighter than air.

Whereas the Wright brothers' aeroplane was powered by propellers, modern aircraft are driven by jet engines. The modern jumbo jet can carry over 400 passengers, fly at speeds of around 900 kilometres per hour and cruise at over 10,000 kilometres above the Earth. Long haul flights can last for up to a whole day! At these speeds and heights, the aircraft cabins need to be pressurised and air-conditioned for passengers and crew to survive. The supersonic airliner, Concorde, could fly even higher and faster, at speeds greater than the speed of sound.

Like many inventions which have changed the world, aeroplanes have been used for destructive as well as peaceful purposes. The Wright brothers offered their 'flying machine' to the US government for military use before World War One. In the Second World War, aircraft were used to bomb cities, which resulted in the death of large numbers of people. Military planes have now been developed which can do remarkable things: some can be refuelled whilst in flight; the Harrier 'jump-jet' can take off and land vertically;

the Stealth bomber is shaped and constructed to make it invisible on the radar screens which follow the flight of aircraft through the skies.

Although there have been designs for helicopters since mediaeval times, the first really practical one did not fly until 1940. Helicopters are slow and use a lot of fuel compared with planes, but their big advantage is that they are easy to manoeuvre in different directions, and can land almost anywhere. Today, helicopters are used by police, ambulance and rescue services 24 hours a day. They cover a variety of vital services from traffic reports and crime fighting to life-saving at sea.

As well as letting us circle the globe, powered flight has enabled humans to explore space for the first time. Spacecraft are driven by powerful rocket engines, which are the only ones which will work in space. Since the first manned flights and the moon landings in the 1960s, spacecraft have been developed that can be used more than once. The Space Shuttle looks more like an aircraft than a rocket. It can carry cargo and crew into space and land back on Earth.

Just over a hundred years after the first powered flight, it is normal to use aeroplanes for holidays and business travel. People watch films, eat meals and sleep whilst these magnificent flying machines take them all over the globe. The world now seems a much smaller place thanks to Orville Wright's wonderful 12-second flight. Will Space shrink in the same way in the future?

HOW AN AIRCRAFT FLIES

A modern jet aircraft can weigh hundreds of tonnes – more than a small herd of elephants. It is also the size of a pretty large building. So how on Earth does it get off the ground?

Try this experiment. Hold a piece of paper with both hands just below your lips, so that it bends downwards, and blow over the top of it. The paper begins to rise slightly. What causes the paper to rise? The answer is that when you blow, you make the air over the top of the paper travel faster, so there is less air pressure. This means the air pressure is greater below the paper where the air is travelling more slowly. The higher pressure below it forces the paper up.

Exactly the same effect enables an aeroplane to fly. Most modern aeroplanes are powered by jet engines which give them a forward push called 'thrust'. As the plane speeds along the runway, air flows past the wings. An aeroplane's wings have a curved shape so that the air above the wing has to travel further and faster than the air below the wing. This causes an upward force called 'lift.' Eventually, when the plane is travelling fast enough, the upward lift is a greater force than the weight of the plane. As a result, the plane rises off the ground. Flaps can be extended in order to make the wings even more curved and so increase the lift further.

Pointed nose and rounded body mean less 'drag'

Engines create forward push called 'thrust'

BRITISH AIRWAYS

Air flowing over and under curved wings create 'lift'

SUPERSONIC CONCORDE TAKING OFF

In order to make the plane travel as fast as possible, designers make its shape streamlined. The nose of the plane is a pointed shape and the body of the plane rounded because this gives less 'drag', or air resistance. The pilot retracts the plane's wheels as soon as possible after take-off to make the aircraft even more streamlined. The aeroplane has a vertical tail fin to stop it wobbling too much and so provide a smoother flight.

Aeroplanes have to keep moving forwards to stay in the air. They also need a long runway for take-off and landing. Helicopters, by contrast, can take off and land vertically almost anywhere. This is because they have rotor blades which spin, rather than wings. Rotating the blades at speed gives the helicopter its lift, rather than the acceleration needed for a runway. Once it is in the air, a helicopter can fly upwards, downwards and sideways, as well as hover. This is because the rotor blades create a downwash of air which forces the machine upwards. Slowing, speeding up or tilting the rotors allows the helicopter to fly in different directions.

A modern aircraft is very carefully designed so that it has powerful enough engines to give it forward thrust, but is not too noisy when it takes off. It must have a streamlined body to reduce drag, but has to be large enough to carry as many passengers as possible and have wings the right shape to give it lift. When all these things are in place, then we have lift-off!

HELICOPTERS ARE OFTEN USED IN SEA RESCUES

The pilot can move the helicopter in different directions and make it hover. He does this by using the control column to change the angle, or 'pitch', of the rotor blades.

The main rotor blades spin at speed to create 'lift'.

The tail rotor blades prevent the helicopter from spinning round in the opposite direction to the main rotor blades.

Mobiles and Messages

For many people in the UK, life would be massively different without a mobile phone. In the past we could talk across long distances only on phones in fixed places: homes, offices, or call boxes. Today, tens of millions of British people own mobiles; we can use these to make calls *wherever* we are.

SAY IT ON SCREEN

With old fixed-place phones we could communicate only by talking; on mobiles we can make *written* contact too. A feature called SMS (Short Message Service) lets us write and send text messages – using the letters and numbers on our phone keypads. British people send and receive around 55 million text messages every day. It is a fast and fun way to keep in touch, since 95% of all messages arrive within 10 seconds.

THE WONDERS OF WAP

WAP mobiles let us communicate in even more ways. Besides linking us to other mobile users, these new phones also link us up to the Internet. Someone with a WAP mobile can now: read and reply to emails; read the latest news headlines; play games online with a friend; check out a bank balance; and shop for CDs or books. A WAP user can even download a favourite piece of music – then use it as a mobile ringtone!

Some new mobiles have built-in cameras. These let us send messages to one another in photo or video form. Meanwhile, on mobiles with joysticks we can play games we have downloaded.

A WHOLE NEW LANGUAGE

Text language is not like the language you read in books or write in school. There are many shorter, quicker ways of typing common words. Instead of typing 'great', you can type 'GR8', for instance. You can also type shorthand versions of whole sentences, like 'g2g2sch' (I've got to go to school) or 'TMB' (Text me back). The way it works is this: you break up the words into sounds and write each sound as small as you can. So 'before' could be 'B4'; 'C' could mean 'see' or 'sea'. Numbers could stand in for the letters they sound like: '1' for 'won', '2' for 'to' or 'two', and so on.

Using letters, numbers and punctuation marks, you can even communicate by typing little faces called 'emoticons' on to the screen. They are called emoticons because they show what emotion you are feeling. For example:
:-) happy; :-(sad; :-0 surprised; :-S unsure; :-* kissy.

The first text message was sent in 1992 – that's 400 years after Shakespeare wrote his plays. If he had written in text language, it might have looked like this. Can you work out what King Richard III is saying?

DICTIONARY TEXT

CUL8R *(phrase)* See you later!

fascia/facia *(noun)* the removable plastic cover for a mobile

hands-free kit *(adjective and noun)* an add-on for your mobile, consisting of headphones and a microphone, that leaves your hands free while you talk

integrated camera *(adjective and noun)* a camera that is built into your mobile, not simply attached to it

sim card *(noun)* your mobile's memory, containing all the information (like friends' numbers) that you have saved; it can be transferred to another mobile when you upgrade

T9 *(noun)* the name given to predictive texting

URBNGR8 *(phrase)* You're being great!

voicemail *(noun)* a mobile's own answering machine. If someone leaves you a voice message, voicemail records it then texts you to tell you about it!

W@UBN@? *(phrase)* What have you been doing?

gggg UK4gg

'A horse, a horse, my kingdom for a horse!'

INDEX